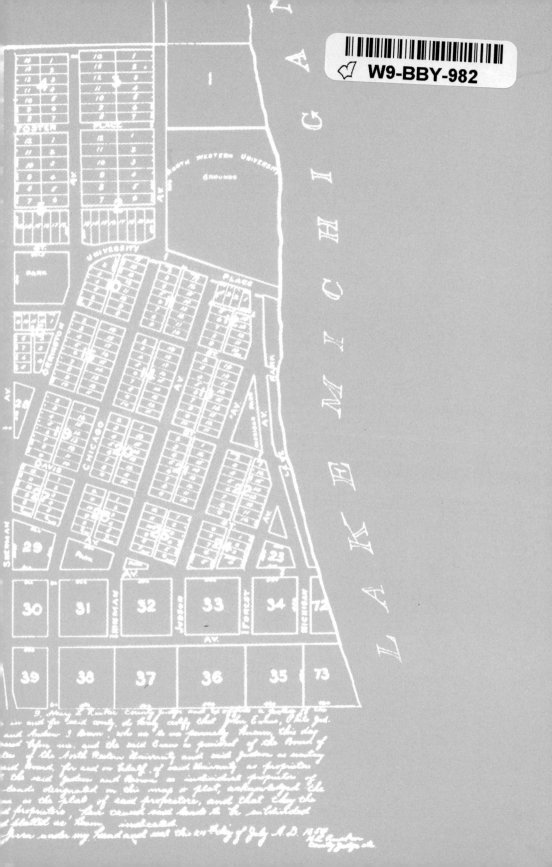

Evanston: 150 Years 150 Places

Second Edition

Design Evanston celebrates
Evanston's notable architecture

Compiled and written by Design Evanston members
Stuart Cohen, Kris Hartzell, Heidrun Hoppe, Laura Saviano and Jack Weiss
Inroduction by Heidrun Hoppe

Designed by Jack Weiss

Edited by Heidrun Hoppe

Published by Design Evanston
designevanston.org

ISBN 978-0-9894593-0-3
ISBN 978-0-9894593-1-0

Cover Photo: Amanda, Wikimedia Commons
Inside Covers: Evanston History Center

Printing and binding: LifeTouch Printing, Loves Park, Illinois
Paper: U Velvet Matte 100lb Text and Cover
Type: Goudy Old Style

Design Evanston

Founded in 1980, Design Evanston is a 501(c)(3) not-for-profit advocacy organization promoting good design in Evanston, Illinois. Design Evanston attracts a wide range of professionals living or working in Evanston, including architects, planners, graphic designers, landscape architects, web designers and industrial designers.

Design Evanston is an active and vocal observer of the city's review process and a supporter of early review of projects for owners and organizations. Since its founding, Design Evanston has prepared design guidelines for the Public Library design competition, sponsored public forums on design excellence and has granted over one hundred awards for completed projects of merit through its Design Evanston Awards program.

Proceeds from the sale of this book support the projects and programs of Design Evanston.

Jack Weiss, President
Design Evanston

Acknowledgments

The following individuals provided nominations for the book: Stuart Cohen, Anne Earle, Bonnie Ford, Jane Grover, Kris Hartzell, Heidrun Hoppe, Nate Kipnis, John Macsai, Mary McWilliams, Dudley Onderdonk, Tom Rajkovich, Laura Saviano, Robert Teska, David VanZanten and Jack Weiss.

Thanks also to Kevin Leonard, Northwestern University archivist, and Lori Osborne, Evanston History Center archivist, for their assistance in locating and approving the use of valuable historic photographs. Our gratitude to Granacki Historic Consultants for providing numerous contemporary photographs of historic homes in the Lakeshore Historic District.

We are indebted to The Richard H. Driehaus Foundation for a matching grant that enabled us to publish this second edition.

Contributors

Our heartfelt thanks to the donors who made the publication of this book possible:

Patron: Design Evanston Board of Directors, Evanston Community Foundation, First Bank & Trust, Optima, Inc.

Donor: Hagerty Altenbernd Family Charitable Fund, Evanston Chamber of Commerce

Sponsor: City of Evanston, Ellen Rockwell Galland, Richard & Elaine Heuberger, NeigerDesign, Ross Barney Architects, Jack Weiss Associates

Friend: Downtown Evanston, Robyn Gabel, Tom & Alison Hofmaier, Paul Lehman/Rhonna Stamm, Smeja Family Foundation, Andrew J. Spatz, Sturm Builders, Inc., Robert B. Teska

Subscriber: Laurie B. Marston, Myefski Architects

Table of Contents

Appendices

The following abbreviations are used throughout the book to identify landmark or award status:
(NR) National Register of Historic Places
(LL) City of Evanston Local Landmark
(DE) Design Evanston Award
(PA) City of Evanston Preservation Award

Introduction

Evanston's built environment both shapes and reflects our city's culture, economy, aesthetics and historical life. In the 150 years since its incorporation, a multitude of buildings, parks, rail lines, monuments and streets have been realized, each adding its bit to what we have become in 2013. Through Design Evanston's *Evanston:150 Years, 150 Places* we seek to inspire residents to reflect on our rich legacy and, through this, to recognize the importance of the built environment in shaping our future.

Our authors consulted many different people and investigated many ideas in arriving at the two basic themes that were used to identify our final list of entries: 1. Is this structure or place architecturally significant, either because of particular design excellence or because it is indicative of trends or milestones in architectural history? 2. Is this structure or place culturally or historically important to Evanston? Taken together, these two strands are points along the living timeline that is Evanston.

Any selection process is bound to leave out important potential entries. We are lucky in Evanston to have many more significant places than could be included in this collection. We were forced to make choices between equals; in some cases one entry serves as representative of a larger notable group. Although we included many places recommended by others, the determination of "in" vs. "out" was the collective decision of the authors alone.

You may notice that the list leans toward residential buildings. Evanston is a city of homes, with our cultural, educational and commercial institutions growing up around those who came—and still come—to this spot to live. Gems of architectural design are often the single-family houses of the well-to-do, and their representation is an important part of this book. We found, however, that the beautifully designed apartment buildings and simple modest homes are truly the connecting fabric of this city; selecting among their great number was a difficult task.

We chose to include some demolished structures that were too important to leave out. We expanded beyond more typical choices and somewhat ducked our "150" restriction by including several appendices: Parks and Open Spaces, Cultural and Commercial Landmarks, Shopping and Cultural Districts, New Deal Art in Evanston and a list of mail-order homes that were constructed here.

The 150 entries in the main body of the book are organized by date built. Original owner or use is given and whether or not the building or place has earned local or national landmark status. Complete records were not always kept for many of the buildings, and historical details are sometimes conflicting. We have attempted to provide as accurate a description as possible within the bounds of available information. A bibliography is included which points toward further reading for anyone interested.

Finally, at the end of the book you will find an index and maps of the four Evanston quadrants with each entry located. We hope you will enjoy walking through your city and seeing many of these notable places for yourself.

Our built environment is the physical legacy of what came before. We live, work, study, play and worship within a history that is living and will continue to evolve for others to record. – *Heidrun Hoppe*

Mulford House "Oakton"
250 Ridge Avenue
Architect unknown
1845 (Demolished 1963)

In about 1845, Major Edward Mulford, Evanston's first permanent resident, moved from a nearby log cabin where he and his family had lived since 1837 into the house at the east end of their 160-acre estate that he named "Oakton." Mulford, who had purchased the land from the U.S. Government about 1841, lived in the house until his death in 1878. The house was later remodeled into a 3-story, 22-room wood and stucco house. Mulford's granddaughter Anna Mulford Brown sold off major portions of the estate and in 1963 the house was demolished to make room for "Mulford House," Evanston's first condominium. Mulford's estate also gave its name to Oakton Street, the estate's northern boundary. In 2004 much of the area once occupied by Mulford's estate became part of the Oakton Historic District and was placed on the National Register of Historic Places. JW

1

Calvary Cemetery Gateway (LL)
401 Chicago Avenue
Architect: James Egan
1859

Not as well known as other Chicago area cemeteries like Rosehill or Graceland, Calvary Cemetery, consecrated in 1859, is the oldest Catholic cemetery in the area. It sits on the lakefront at Sheridan Road, with its main entrance on Chicago Avenue and its rear entrance directly east on Sheridan. A wide road connects the two gates. Originally, a small lagoon lay in between, roughly two-thirds of the way from the east end, but it was filled in to create shrine sections. This dramatically changed the appearance of the cemetery, as did the loss of many trees to Dutch Elm disease in the 1960s. The west entrance of Calvary is through a large limestone gate with three arches designed by James Egan (who is buried in Calvary). The center arch is surmounted by a triangle in the Gothic style to represent the Greek letters Alpha and Omega. JW

Willard House (NR, LL, PA)
1728–1730 Chicago Avenue
Builder: Josiah Willard
1865
(Addition 1880–81)

Frances Willard's father Josiah admired landscape architect Andrew Jackson Downing and built a Gothic Revival house at 1728 Chicago Avenue based on a pattern in Downing's book, *Victorian Cottage Residences*. Willard's house, with decorative vergeboard and carved finials, is one of only two vertical board-and-batten houses remaining in Evanston. The north addition was built in 1880–81 for Frances Willard's widowed sister-in-law and children. From 1879 until her death in 1898 Frances Willard led the Woman's Christian Temperance Union in work for social reform, including woman suffrage. Willard willed her house to the WCTU, which in 1900 moved its headquarters into the addition and turned the 1865 house into a museum, believed to be the oldest house museum in America honoring the life work of a woman. The building was designated a National Historic Landmark in 1965. SC

University Hall (LL)
Northwestern University
1897 Sheridan Road
Architect: Gurdon P. Randall
1869

As the first architecturally significant building in the area, University Hall established Gothic Revival as the style for Northwestern's campus and the town, reflecting the religious foundation of the university. Ideally sited on high ground at the curving entrance to campus, this 3-1/2 story structure is highlighted by a 120-foot tower at the southwest corner. Designed by the prestigious architect Gurdon P. Randall, it is built of Joliet limestone, as is Chicago's Water Tower. This iconic building took three years to build and originally held classrooms, lecture halls, dorm rooms, the library, a chapel and a natural history museum. The class of 1879 added the tower's clock, followed by the bells from the class of 1880. Long the focal point of campus, it was the highest structure in Evanston for many years. The pride of the community, Frances Willard declared it "a poem in stone." **KH**

701 Forest Avenue (NR, LL)
Architect unknown
c1872

This house with its corner tower falls into one of six subtypes of Italianate called the Towered Italianate or Italian Villa. It is one of the best examples of its kind on the North Shore. It retains its signature square corner tower and is the only Italian Villa house in Evanston with its tower intact. Others had towers that have since been removed. The house has several features characteristic of the Italian Villa style. The overall shape is irregular, reflecting an informal floor plan inside. The house has two stories, culminating in a shallow roof. The roof's deep cornice is supported by paired decorative brackets that are connected by a row of tooth-like dentils, hanging pendants and paneled frieze. Tall windows have triangular-pedimented window hoods. The three-story tower features narrow triple windows on the third floor. Another typical feature is the elaborate wood cornice under the main hipped roof. JW

First Baptist Church of Evanston (NR, LL)
(now Lake Street Church)
607 Lake Street
Architect: Cass Chapman
1873

Evanston Baptist Church–now called Lake Street Church–was founded in 1858 by Frances Gano and Edward and Rebecca Mulford, among others. The first church was built at the northeast corner of Church and Hinman. In 1872 the congregation commissioned the current building at Chicago Avenue and Lake Street. Work on the Gothic Revival brick structure progressed slowly because of the financial panic of 1873. The building was finally dedicated in 1875 and is the oldest of the four churches built around Raymond Park. The verticality of the design is emphasized by slender, pointed-arch windows and the tall steeple topping the bell tower on the southeast corner. Two structures currently comprise Lake Street Church: the 1873 building by Cass Chapman and a 1920 Gothic Revival addition by Tallmadge & Watson. The 1920 addition at 1458 Chicago Avenue includes administrative and educational functions and is also architecturally significant. JW

Grosse Point Light Station (NR, LL)
2535 Sheridan Road
Architect: Orlando M. Poe
1874

Perhaps Evanston's most iconic structure, the Grosse Point Light Station was built in 1874 by the U.S. Government at a cost of $35,000. The tapering shaft of the lighthouse stands 113 feet tall and is 25 feet in diameter at its base. The structure is supported on piles. The exterior walls, built of brick, received a thick coating of concrete in 1914. The lighthouse is connected to the 8-room "keeper's" house facing Sheridan Road. Two fog signal houses were constructed in 1880 to house steam sirens that were later removed. An account, not accepted by historians, holds that during the Civil War Confederate soldiers removed the lens from a lighthouse on the Florida coast to thwart Union approaches. The buried lens was found by the Union army, brought north, and installed in Evanston's lighthouse. Decommissioned in 1934, the land and keeper's house were given to the City of Evanston in 1935. The lighthouse tower was deeded to the city in 1941. SC

Fountain Square

Sherman Avenue & Davis Street
Architect unknown
1876
(Restoration 1976 by Barton-Aschman)

*Photos: (above) Evanston History Center
(below) Chain12, Flickr*

The current Fountain Square is the third iteration of Evanston's focal urban space located on the triangular site between Orrington and Sherman Avenues and Church Street. Known officially as the Bicentennial Fountain, the most recent design is a triangular complex of three fountains and pools, with steps, angled ramps, ample built-in seating and three brick columns memorializing the names of Evanstonians who died in all of this nation's wars. The current fountain and plaza supersedes the 1949 War Memorial Fountain designed by Hubert Burnham, son of Evanston architect Daniel Burnham. The original Centennial Fountain, a three-tiered cast iron design by J.L. Mott Iron Works, New York, was dedicated on July 4, 1876. In 1912 it was replaced with a replica, which stood for many years in front of the Old City Hall. The deteriorating fountain was taken down, stored, and ultimately re-dedicated in the Merrick Rose Garden on July 4, 1951. SC

Kedzie House
1514 Ridge Avenue
Architect: Cass Chapman
1881 (Demolished 1967)

This stately home was one of the foremost of the grand mansions that stood along Evanston's ridge. The natural high ground served as an early trail through the region and in the late 1880s it became the premiere street on which to build. The striking Italianate villa was notable for its oversized 84-foot square central tower soaring above the 2-1/2 story house. The architect was Cass Chapman, who had also designed the second First Methodist Church (now demolished) and the First Baptist Church (now Lake Street Church) and was known for his lofty towers. Constructed of buff-colored brick, the Kedzie House was wrapped with a double-columned expansive porch. The windows were topped with decorative limestone hoods. The interior had a marble-floored entry hall, stained glass and a massive black walnut stair. John Kedzie was an influential developer in the area. Kedzie Street in Evanston and Kedzie Avenue in Chicago are named for him. KH

Holabird House
1500 Oak Avenue
Architect: Holabird & Roche
1883 (Demolished 1969)

William Holabird moved to Evanston and designed a house for his family in 1883. Sadly, it was demolished in 1969. Holabird was a partner in the architectural firm of Holabird & Roche, which became one of Chicago's largest and most important architectural firms. Holabird's house was typical of the period with its large front-facing gable, symmetrical bay windows and large ground floor entry porch. Perhaps the most unusual feature was the decorative fretwork that entirely covered the gable end above the third floor. Holabird and his partner Martin Roche had worked together for William LeBaron Jenney, considered the father of the steel frame skyscraper. Holabird was a graduate of West Point; his father, who was the U.S. Army's Quartermaster General, was responsible for awarding his son's firm the commission to design Fort Sheridan. Although Holabird & Roche are remembered as commercial architects they designed seven houses that were built in Evanston. SC

1400 Wesley Avenue (LL)
Architect unknown
1888
(Renovation 2012 by Lineworks, Ltd.)

1400 Wesley is an example of a building vernacular commonly, although perhaps mistakenly, referred to as a "Luxembourg House," so named for the immigrants from Luxembourg and Germany who settled in Evanston and Skokie. This house stands just outside the Ridge Historic District and is a reminder of early times. A number of these Evanston houses featured a brick first story designed to withstand the flooding common in the then low-lying swampland west of Ridge (which sometimes required travel by boat). Early stories claim that tools and, at times, animals were kept in the lower level and that the family lived above. At the time it was built, modern wood framing with studs and mass-produced nails had replaced the older mortise-and-tenon techniques and hand-wrought nails. Some of these buildings featured an exterior stair to the second floor; this stair can be seen in another example of this house type nearby at 1501 Lake Street. **HH**

Dearborn Observatory (LL)
Northwestern University
2131 Tech Drive
Architect: Cobb & Frost
1889

The Chicago Astronomical Society signed an agreement with Northwestern University in 1887 to bring a telescope with an 18-1/2 inch lens–the largest in the world at the time–to Evanston. The architecture firm of Cobb & Frost designed the $25,000 Dearborn Observatory, which was dedicated in 1889. In the summer of 1939 the building had to be moved to make way for the construction of the Technological Institute. The three-month move to the new location took twenty-six men, a tractor and two teams of horses. The Observatory experienced another metamorphosis in August 1997, when it received a new 38-foot aluminum dome. It was also equipped with a new electronic gear system to manipulate the dome and telescope, which had previously been moved by a hand crank. The building at the base of Dearborn Observatory's dome, renovated in 1985, holds a research and historical library with a reading room on the first floor. JW

Mayfair Cutoff

2030 Green Bay Road
Builder: The Junction Railroad Company
(subsidiary of the Chicago & North Western Railway)
1889
(Bridge abutment c1937)

Photo: GoogleMaps

Evanstonians may notice the vestige of a diagonal line running from Simpson St. and Green Bay Rd. southwest to Howard St. near McCormick Blvd. The line appears and disappears, forming triangular lots and raised embankments along the way. This is the path of the former rail spur known as the Mayfair Cutoff. By the 1880s passenger travel along what is now the Metra line was frequently slowed by freight trains using the same tracks. To alleviate this, the Mayfair Cutoff, named for its terminus at the Mayfair Junction in Chicago, was built to carry freight through unsettled land. Hoping to lure residents to the open land, however, Evanston required the railway to include passenger depots at Emerson, Greenwood and the Weber Train Yard near Oakton. By 1910 the Emerson and Greenwood passenger stops were discontinued, but trains carried Weber employees until 1958. Freight travelled the spur until the 1960s; it was abandoned completely in the 1980s. **HH**

Orr House (NR, LL)
202 Greenwood Street
Architect: Joseph Lyman Silsbee
1889

Arthur Orr was a shipping magnate who married the daughter of Rev. Noyes of Evanston's First Presbyterian Church. A friend of neighbor Daniel Burnham, Orr commissioned him to design several buildings in Evanston. However, for his own home he chose Silsbee to design this immense Shingle Style home with its enormous gambrel roof and clapboard siding. Silsbee, an adept practitioner of this style, later employed both George Maher and Frank Lloyd Wright at the start of their careers.

Wright's 1892 McArthur Residence references this house. The cascading roof of Orr's house envelops the second story and is rhythmically punctuated by four prominently pedimented dormer windows. The raised freestone foundation is carried through the roof by the asymmetrically positioned chimney. Rounded lateral bays, curvilinear muntins and a decorative arched entry pediment supported by stone columns compose the Classical elements of the house. **KH**

1401–1407 Elmwood Avenue (NR, LL)
Architect: Stephen A. Jennings
1890

Photo (above): Stuart Cohen
(below): Thshriver, Wikimedia Commons

These four buff brick two-story row houses skillfully combine the picturesque features of both the Queen Anne and Shingle styles popular in the 1890s. Their designer, Stephen Jennings, was the architect of many of Evanston's architecturally significant homes. The four houses were mirrored about a center, which has a large projecting gable and separate projecting shed-roofed wood porches for the two center units. Both the gabled and hipped roofs extend forward on timber brackets, giving the individual units prominence even though they repeat symmetrically. The two corner houses are accentuated by arched recessed entryways, projecting hipped roofs and large second-floor corner windows. These windows are remarkable in that they foreshadow an important feature of 20th century architecture, the corner window. Here the corner has a thin round classical column. SC

15

Emmanuel Methodist Church (NR, LL)

1401 Oak Avenue
Architect: Burnham & Root
1890

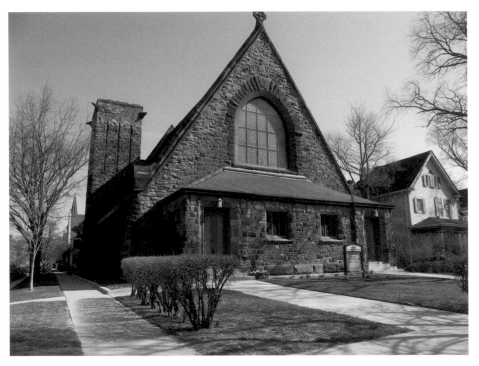

Emmanuel Methodist Church, an offshoot of First Methodist Church in Evanston, was established in 1890 to serve the west side of town. Designed by Burnham & Root, it is largely attributed to John Welbourn Root and is considered one of his last works, finished after his death in 1891. The church is built of beautiful Lake Superior red sandstone, said to have the lamination of marble. Built at a cost of $60,000, it is reminiscent of the style of architect H.H. Richardson with its monolithic massing and use of rock-faced stone. The tower is unusually placed at the rear of the building, at the junction of the assembly hall and chapel. It once rose to 135 feet, but the towering four-sided, flared-eave steeple was hit by lightning, burned and was removed. The interior is simple, presaging the Prairie School, and once had a translucent glass ceiling that flooded the chapel with natural light. **KH**

Farwell House (NR, LL)
1433 Hinman Avenue
Architect: John Van Osdel
1890

One of the last designs by John Van Osdel, Chicago's first architect, this intriguing Queen Anne composition in red brick was built for Simeon Farwell, the brother of noted Chicago mercantilist John Farwell. On a corner lot, the house presents two primary façades to the streets. The prominent northern bay is topped by a pargetted gable and enhanced by elaborate foliated scrollwork. A high conical tower on the south end balances the northern bay with its round of banded windows. The battered columns of the front porch are reminiscent of Egyptian motifs. The peaked roof is highlighted by an unusual elongated eyebrow dormer and supported by a bracketed eave. The entrance is on the north façade and is accentuated by the tall triple leaded-glass windows soaring above it on the second floor. **KH**

Jernegan House (NR, LL)
1144 Michigan Avenue
Architect: Enock Hill Turnock
1890

Charles Jernegan was a member of the Chicago Board of Trade. His family's Evanston home is one of the finest Queen Anne/ Shingle Style houses in the Chicago area. Among the house's extraordinary features are the double bay windows suspended above the large wraparound porch and the expression of the main stair by a wall of windows which follow the stair's ascent on the north side. Architect Enock Turnock worked in the Chicago office of William LeBaron Jenney (considered the father of the steel frame skyscraper), after which he returned to Elkhart, Indiana, where he practiced for most of his career. He is best known for the Brewster Apartments in Chicago, a building in which all the apartments are accessed from iron and glass catwalks in a glass covered atrium. The shingled coach house, a new structure at the west end of the Jernegan property, was designed by the Chicago firm of DLK Architecture, Inc. SC

St. Mary's Church (NR, LL, DE)
1012 Lake Street
Architect: Stephen A. Jennings
1890
(Interior renovation 2004 by Torvik Associates)

The Catholic parish of St. Mary's was founded in Evanston in 1865. This is the third church building on the original site at Lake and Oak and was designed by parishioner and popular Evanston architect Stephen Alston Jennings. Built of rock-faced Lemont limestone in the Victorian Gothic style, it employs many of Jennings' signature elements, including the high, narrow arched windows. This stylistic detail is repeated in the open arches under the flared eaves of the steeples atop the twin 100-foot spires that flank the entrance and are topped with open arched belfries. The tall, narrow steeples are capped by stone crosses, which are repeated at the peaks of the many gables. The rose window over the entry depicts the Eight Beatitudes and overlooks the nave from above the choir loft. The interior was extensively renovated by Torvik Associates in 2004. KH

318-320 Dempster Street (LL)
Architect: D.H. Burnham & Co.
1892

Photo: Granacki Historic Consultants

Evanston has a number of handsome double houses among its streets of single-family homes. They are frequently indistinguishable from the adjacent houses and often have separate entrances set back from the front of the house on either side with wraparound porches. This residence is easily recognizable as a double house because the entry doors to each unit are paired at the center of the street façade. Where many of Evanston's double houses have front-facing gables or other roof configurations that read as two homes, 318-320 Dempster has a single gambrel roof that unifies the two units, as do the evenly spaced roof dormers. 318-320 Dempster was designed by Daniel Burnham as an investment property for his friends and fellow Evanston residents, H. R. Post and William Brown. Burnham's firm designed Brown's house, as well as the former Miller School one block to the west (now the Chiaravalle Montessori School). sc

1209-1217 Maple Avenue (NR, LL)
Architect: Holabird & Roche
1892

Among the earliest multifamily buildings in Evanston, these Victorian row houses were carefully designed to fit into Evanston's streets of single-family homes. (They can be compared to 1101–1113 Maple one block to the south.) The architect was William Holabird, a prominent Evanston resident whose architectural firm designed Evanston's original city hall. The single building at 1209-1217 Maple is actually five three-story brick houses, each with its own covered entry porch and with shared party walls. The end and center houses have projecting second floor wood bay windows. Above these are gable ends, each finished with different trim and siding and with large double windows. The center house has a gambrel roof with a three-part Palladian window that marks the center of the entire row. These houses assert their individuality while also suggesting that the building was designed to be seen as a coherent whole. SC

Bradley House (NR, LL)
1745 Hinman Avenue
Architect: Bosworth & Chase
1892

Perhaps Evanston's most stylistically eclectic house, this stucco and half-timber house was built by Charles F. Bradley, professor of New Testament Exegesis at the Garrett Biblical Institute. Featured in the very first issue of *House Beautiful* magazine in 1896, the house was described as "French Gothic." Its roof line and circular stair tower suggest a mini chateau, while the house's half-timbered features suggest French Norman or English Tudor sources. The house was designed by William Chase of Boston, who was Bradley's brother-in-law. Other prominent residents over the years included Benjamin Crawford, president of the National Biscuit Company (Nabisco). Inside, the carved dark-stained woodwork, ceiling beams and hand carved fireplace mantels live up to the house's picturesque exterior. SC

Low House (NR, LL)
1560 Oak Avenue
Architect: Stephen A. Jennings
1892 (Destroyed 2011)

The same year St. Mary's Church was built, parishioners John and Jennie Low commissioned Jennings to design this elaborate home. This stunning example of his work was unfortunately destroyed by fire in 2011. A symphony of elements favored by the architect came together in the orchestration of this house, from the turret with its flared conical roof to the rusticated stone front porch. Many similar stylistic elements may still be seen in the Jennings-designed Jones House at 1232 Ridge Avenue.

Of particular interest was the steeply pitched bell-curve gable with its arched and deep-set window, a hallmark of Jennings' style. These graceful curves were echoed in the sweeping roof of the entrance pavilion. The pediment over the porch stairs carried a scrolled and foliated design. For over fifty years it housed the St. Mary's-affiliated Catholic Women's Club. It was recognized by the Illinois State Historical Survey as a significant structure. **KH**

Noyes Street School (LL)
(now Noyes Cultural Center)
927 Noyes Street
Architect: D. H. Burnham & Co.
1892

This is the second of four Evanston schools designed by Daniel Burnham. Built of Milwaukee Cream City brick, its verticality is enhanced by the tall narrow windows. The central section is flanked by two lateral bays that are set slightly back from the central section. A tall, wood battened cornice meets the roof rafters of the slightly overhanging eaves. The classrooms were positioned on the north and south sides of a wide axial hall. The first northern addition, with its large arched entry, was designed by Burnham's nephew Ernest Woodyatt in 1902. Further revisions were executed by Edgar Ovet Blake in 1914. The gymnasium and auditorium wing were added in 1949, designed by Perkins and Will. Larimer School at Oak and Crain was the same design, but was demolished in 1936. Declining enrollment closed the school in the 1970s and it was converted to use as a cultural arts center in 1980. **KH**

Old City Hall

Northwest corner Sherman Avenue & Davis Street
Architect: Holabird & Roche
1892 (Demolished)

Originally known as Evanston Village Hall, this building was also intended to house the police department, fire department and the public library. Built at the important civic location of Fountain Square, it housed council chambers on the first floor with the library above. The building suffered from financial problems and construction delays; it never housed the fire department and with the incorporation of Evanston as a city in 1892, it was determined to be too small.

(Evanston had incorporated as a town in 1863.) Evanston resident William Holabird designed the building in the Romanesque style popularized by H.H. Richardson, whose architectural work includes libraries and government buildings throughout the country. Heavy stone masonry, arched windows on the first and second floor and a range of dormer windows distinguished Old City Hall, as did circular corner towers with decorative brick patterning. SC

1301–03/1305–07 Judson Avenue (NR, LL)
Architect: Sidney Smith
1894

These twin four-flat buildings were the earliest multifamily structures in a solely residential area. Designed to blend into the surrounding neighborhood of Queen Anne and Shingle Style homes, the structures nevertheless met with local opposition. To give the appearance of a single-family home the paired entry doors are under one front-pedimented portico. Employing a variety of exterior materials, the raised basement and foundations are of rough-cut limestone, the first floors are red brick and the second floors are shingled. The high, hipped roofs have large cross gables. On the front façades, the large single-pane windows are topped with leaded-glass fixed transom windows. The rounded second-story oriels have diamond-paned casement windows and the center gables have small twin pedimented aedicules, in keeping with the era's penchant for combining different types and styles. Wrought iron light fixtures in a gargoyle motif flank the entrance doors. **KH**

Anthony House (NR, LL)
225 Hamilton Street
Architect: Pond & Pond
1894

Photo: Inland Architect

Superior Court Judge Elliot Anthony, a prominent Chicago lawyer, was one of the founders of the Republican Party in Illinois and served as president of the Illinois Bar Association. An avid book collector whose house was destroyed in the Great Chicago Fire of 1871, Anthony built this fireproof house in Evanston in 1895. His new library, the main room of the house, originally had a sprinkler system and metal shutters. A story and a half tall, the library, on the west side of the house, has clerestory windows above walls of bookcases. Anthony's brick and shingle Queen Anne house was designed by the Chicago firm of Pond and Pond. The Pond brothers designed many fashionable residences but were best known for Jane Addams' Hull House and their interest in social reform. Irving Pond served as national president of the American Institute of Architects and was the author of a number of books on architecture. SC

Dawes House (NR, LL)
(now Evanston History Center)
225 Greenwood Street
Architect: Henry Edwards-Ficken
1894

Photos: Evanston History Center

Occupied by the Evanston Historical Society since 1957, this house was previously the residence of Calvin Coolidge's vice president Charles Gates Dawes, who received the Nobel Peace Prize in 1925 for his work restructuring Germany's war reparations after WWI. The brick and sandstone French Chateau house was originally designed for Northwestern University professor and business manager Robert Dickenson Sheppard, who built this grand home convinced that he would one day be Northwestern's president. However, Sheppard was forced to resign upon discovery of some financial improprieties. The designer, New York society architect Henry Edwards-Ficken had worked for Richard Morris Hunt, the Paris-trained architect responsible for making French architecture popular in the United States. Predominantly French, the lavish interior combines both French and English decorative details. The Evanston History Center is open to the public. SC

First Presbyterian Church (NR, LL)

1427 Chicago Avenue
Architect: Daniel H. Burnham
1894

After losing their first two wooden churches to fire, the Presbyterian congregation chose Joliet limestone for their third edifice. Under the direction of Reverend Noyes, Daniel Burnham was given the commission. It is designed primarily in the Italian Renaissance style with some Gothic elements but minimal ornamentation. The rusticated limestone building has a red clay tile roof with two immense cross gables that embrace soaring and elaborate stained glass windows. The prominent tower on the northwest corner is 24 feet square and 120 feet tall with an open belfry of paired Gothic arches. Its shallow hipped roof was once topped with a large weathervane. The sanctuary seats over one thousand; its roof is supported by massive rib vaults and trusses of red oak. Henry Wheelock designed the additions in 1925, including the narthex and the meeting hall. The chapel was added in 1948. **KH**

Jones House (NR, LL)
1232 Ridge Avenue
Architect: Stephen A. Jennings
1894

Considered the apogee of this prolific Evanston architect's Queen Anne residences in Evanston, the Jones House is a picturesque extravaganza in stone. This 3-1/2 story monolithic structure in grey rock-faced granite is defined by its two corner turrets and steeply pitched, sweeping central gable. It is highlighted by Jennings' typical narrow, arched inset window. The central section is defined by a succession of rooflines cascading to the expansive front porch with its geometric stone balustrade.

The later addition of a porch on the south façade mimics that of the front. The north turret is polygonal with a sectional roof and third story open loggia. The south tower is rounded, with a conical roof. The interior continues the grandiosity, including massive stone fireplaces and a black walnut stairway, which once held a pipe organ on the landing. William Jones was a partner with fellow Evanstonian Charles Deering in International Harvester. **KH**

2444-2450 Pioneer Road (LL)
Architect: Robert C. Spencer
1895

This grouping of three picturesque cottages represents a significant development in modern suburban architecture. Commissioned by local developer, realtor and alderman Charles Wightman, Spencer also designed a plan to subdivide the irregular lot and give each house a private yard and alley access. The cottages received much attention and critical acclaim. Utilizing essentially similar floor plans, the exterior of each house is unique. The center house most clearly expresses the emerging ethos of the Prairie School with its shallow hipped roof and raised string course, giving it a degree of horizontality and simplicity. The interiors reflect the move away from the high and narrow Victorian methodology to a more subtle and accessible scale. Spencer was justifiably proud of their success as affordable houses with creative integrity. The center house was a model for one of a series of doll houses based on significant architecture. **KH**

Annie May Swift Hall (LL, DE, PA)
Northwestern University
1920 Campus Drive
Architect: Charles Ayars
1895
(Restoration 2008 by Harboe Architects)

Meat-packing magnate Gustavus Swift helped fund this building for Northwestern's Cumnock School of Oratory. A romantic ensemble of Venetian Gothic and Romanesque design, it was named for Swift's daughter Annie May. She had been a student in the School of Oratory but had died tragically young. The Lemont limestone base supports a mélange of Roman brick and terracotta with a red clay tile hipped roof. The design is delineated by brick string courses and geometric motifs created by bricks set at unusual angles. The third story is distinguished by a variegated diamond pattern. As the home of the School of Oratory, later the School of Speech and now of Communication, it housed classrooms and a once state-of-the-art auditorium. It was purportedly the only building devoted to a speech school in the world at the time. Ayars was a native Evanstonian and second generation architect who built many homes in Evanston. **KH**

Burnet House (NR, LL)
1228 Forest Avenue
Architect: Franklin Burnham
1896

Photo: Inland Architect

Shingle Style and Queen Anne houses are usually associated with east coast architecture. Here, some of the best examples were designed by J. L. Silsbee, Frank Lloyd Wright's first employer, and by Franklin Burnham. Burnham (no relation to Daniel Burnham) began his career designing the train station and a number of homes for Kenilworth founder and developer Joseph Sears. This house was built for the Burnet family, but its most famous resident was Charles Gates Dawes, vice president under Calvin Coolidge, who lived in the house from 1904 to 1909. The house features a beautiful wraparound porch with Classical ionic columns, dentil moldings and a shallow archway marking the entrance. The arch is repeated over the second floor windows and in the third floor Palladian window centered on the flat end of the house's gambrel roof. The stairway and all the woodwork on the ground floor are dark-stained mahogany. SC

Hunt House (NR, LL)
1627 Wesley Avenue
Architect: Myron Hunt
1896

Photo: Jack Weiss

Built by architect Myron Hunt for himself, this subtle yet extraordinary house is a progenitor of the nascent Prairie School movement. The design employs many of the compositional elements that were later considered hallmarks of the style: prominent hipped roof, low overhanging eaves, raised string course, lateral porches and wide and banded windows. The dark, shingled exterior enhances the simplified linear massing. Hunt utilized various levels and ceiling heights within the house to create a sense of spatial distinction and flow. Quartersawn oak paneling and trim and a cross-axial plan combine to create a harmonious experience. This was the third of over 30 residences in Evanston designed by Hunt. One of the original four architects with offices in Chicago's Steinway Hall (along with Perkins, Spencer and Wright), Hunt left a legacy of Prairie houses in Evanston before moving to southern California in 1903. The dormer was a later addition. **KH**

Howe House (NR, LL)
1800 Asbury Avenue
Architect: Pond & Pond
1897

This midsized Georgian house was designed for Charles M. Howe, an assistant manager at the Allis Chalmers Company. Howe's architects, Pond & Pond, were one of Chicago's most progressive architectural firms. The house was unusual for the firm, and it is unusual when compared to most Georgian houses, which are typically bilaterally symmetrical with center entrances. Irving Pond instead used a complex composition of windows to subvert the symmetry, placing the elegant Classical entry porch off center and expressing the stair and stair landing with a tall arched-top window. While Howe must have asked for a "Georgian" exterior, the house's classicism stops at the front door. Original photographs published in *The Inland Architect and News Record* show an Arts and Crafts dining room with natural oak wainscoting, an Arts and Crafts mantel and William Morris-style wallpaper. SC

White House (NR, LL, PA)
1307–13 Ridge Avenue
Architect: Myron Hunt
1897

Hunt's most recognized work, this double house for the widow of lawyer Hugh White and her niece is sited at a prominent intersection on the brow of the ridge. Mirroring the same floor plan as Hunt's own house on Wesley, the two plans combine into one linear whole. The impressive hipped roofs rise over red brick masonry construction, emphasizing the horizontality of the massing with their visual weight. The open two-story loggia is supported by heavy timbers over masonry piers with massive curved supporting brackets. The rear façade dramatically descends the slope of the hill. Intricately patterned geometric leaded art glass is repeated throughout the house and in the towering triple windows on the eastern stair landings. Frank Lloyd Wright and Marion Mahony Griffin have both been erroneously cited as contributors, but the design speaks to Hunt's intrinsic mastery of the genre. The southern porch was designed by Ernest Mayo in 1903. **KH**

Hinman Avenue School/Miller School (NR)

(now Chiaravalle Montessori School)
425 Dempster Street
Architect: D.H. Burnham & Co.
1898

When the new Hinman Avenue School building opened in November 1898 it was front page news in the Evanston newspaper. Built of red brick on a limestone base, this Neoclassical building was considered the finest and most technologically advanced of all the schools in Evanston. The strong cornice with its dentils, egg and dart trim and scrolled brackets is of white glazed terracotta tile. Alternating foliate-patterned tiles surround the arched fanlights over the two entrances.

The windows are nearly fourteen feet tall, providing maximum light to the eight original classrooms. Three ornamented limestone balconettes, supported with elegantly scrolled masonry brackets, once graced the second story. Removed and replaced with concrete slabs, the locations are still discernable over the doorways. Sweeping scrolled stone and brick balustrades frame the entry stairs. The eastern bay on the southern façade was a later addition. **KH**

Pirie House (NR, LL, DE)
1330 Church Street
Architect: Myron Hunt
1898

An exceptional example of Hunt's work during his early innovative phase is the house he designed for John T. Pirie, Jr., one of the heirs of the Carson, Pirie, Scott Company. This remarkable composition of geometric shapes is particularly notable for the repetition of its triangular gables and dormers and the assertive pitch of the porch roofs. The theme is enhanced by the abundance of beautiful diamond-paned leaded glass windows bordered with intricate orthogonal designs. Built on Hunt's own subdivided property, the house embraces the corner site with its linear northern façade. The exterior is sheathed in dark brown cedar shingles that serve to harmoniously unify the angulated rhythms. The interior boasted an impressive library with a high vaulted ceiling. Featured in many architectural publications and exhibitions, the house brought acclaim to Hunt's prolific Evanston career and helped establish his reputation as an avant-garde architect. **KH**

The Boylston (NR, LL)
614 Clark Street
Architect: Myron Hunt
1899

This six-flat apartment building is one of the handsomest Georgian Revival buildings in Evanston and one of its oldest existing apartment houses. Its very name suggests the Georgian buildings of Boston's Boylston Street. Myron Hunt, an Evanston resident, is remembered as a Prairie School architect, but this building reflects the range of his talent as well as the classical architectural training he would have received. Along with the delicate pedimented entry porch, two tiny second floor bay windows give the flat front façade three-dimensional relief. The most unusual features are the windows that flank the doorway. These are set in a two-story-high arch of painted wood and project forward. Within the arch, the Georgian "spray" windows on the second floor form a unique variant on a classic Palladian window. These repeat on the east and west sides of the building, which are also finished in red face brick. sc

Gross House (NR, LL)
1100 and 1106 Oak Avenue
Architect: William Carbys Zimmerman
1901

Photo (above): Stuart Cohen
(below): GoogleMaps

These two speculatively built houses are joined only by the gate to a breezeway between them. Their backs are identical but their front façades are not, having two gable ends that are treated differently in shape, width and number of windows. The overall arrangement of windows in each house is different and the canopies over the entry doors are different. The shingles and diamond-pane leaded glass windows unify the two designs. Atypical of the Shingle Style, these houses combine Tudor and Classical elements. The houses were designed for Anna Rew Gross, a lawyer, by William Carbys Zimmerman, who designed nine houses in Evanston between 1897 and 1925, including the Warren house on the lakefront and the Gross' Colonial shingled house at 1104 Ridge. Anna Gross was the founder and first president of the Garden Club of Evanston and was behind the Club's establishment of the Shakespeare Garden at Northwestern University. SC

40

Marywood Academy (NR, PA)
(now Lorraine H. Morton Civic Center)
2100 Ridge Avenue
Architect: Henry Schlacks
1901
(Addition 1925)

Marywood High School (aka Marywood Academy) was opened in 1915 by the Sisters of Providence of St. Mary-of-the-Woods in this four-story Georgian Revival building formerly known as Visitation Academy. Architect Henry Schlacks designed many Catholic churches and schools in the Chicago area, most of Gothic design. A gymnasium that included a pool was added in 1922; another four-story wing built in 1925 housed classrooms, a cafeteria, dining rooms, music studios and dormitories. Marywood, a girls' school, placed special emphasis on college prep courses with the result that more than 80% of its students went on to college. Enrollment peaked at 531 in 1964-65, and the school closed in the spring of 1970. In 1979 it became the home of the Evanston Civic Center. In 2009 the Civic Center was renamed to honor Evanston's mayor who was retiring after 16 years. JW

41

The Melwood (NR, LL)
1201–13 Michigan/205–07 Hamilton
Architect: Wilmore Alloway
1901

The construction of this multifamily building created consternation in the local community because it was the first apartment house in this area of single-family homes. Its name combines the last names of developers James Meloy and Henry Lockwood. Chicago architect Wilmore Alloway chose a refined Georgian style of pale red brick with limestone ornamentation. The long façade facing the park-like esplanade has seven gracefully curved bays articulated by limestone pilasters. A strong dentiled cornice wraps the building, topped by a brick and limestone parapet. Each entrance is enhanced by a large fanlight and sidelights with curvilinear muntins. In a quirky departure from the strong Classical references, the capitals of the engaged columns at the entry doors reflect architect H.H. Richardson's work, a more modern motif. The tiled entry halls have pale marble wainscoting and stairs with balustrades of intricate cast and wrought iron. **KH**

Patten House
1426 Ridge Avenue
Architect: George Maher
1901 (Demolished)

The beautiful wrought iron fence and stone steps are all that remain of James Patten's monumental mansion on Ridge Avenue. The granite-faced structure was a unique work of architecture distinguished by its simple form and abstracted Classical elements. George Washington Maher was one of a group of progressive architects who focused national attention on Chicago architecture at the beginning of the twentieth century. Patten was mayor of Evanston from 1901 to 1905 and a successful grain broker. He became known as the "Wheat King" after cornering the wheat market in 1909, reputedly making two million dollars in one day. Patten was president of Northwestern University's Board of Trustees and donated the Patten Gymnasium (now demolished), also designed by George Maher. Patten donated his home to Northwestern and in 1938 the University sold it to Hemphill & Associates to make way for speculative houses. SC

Washington School (LL)
914 Ashland Avenue
Architect: Patton, Fisher & Miller
1901

Specializing in educational institutions, Patton, Fisher and Miller established their reputation with The Main building at Armour Institute of Technology, now Illinois Institute of Technology. Built of Roman brick and trimmed in Bedford limestone, Washington School was designed with four rectangular sections set at oblique angles to a fifth centralized rectangular hall. A curved colonnade establishes the entry and is articulated with five arches topped with a large, gold-hued Palladian window. A third-story band of Classical windows and a low conical roof complete the pinnacle of this central turret. The low hipped roof of red clay tile and the balanced composition of the windows in the classrooms continue the Renaissance motif. The building received wide public recognition for its design and its innovative use of color on the interiors, along with the latest technology in environmental controls and marble appointments. Later additions were designed by Perkins & Will. **KH**

The Evanston Apartments (NR, LL)
502–12 Lee/936–40 Hinman
Architect: John Atchison
1902

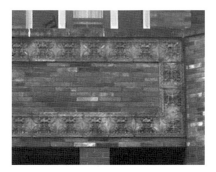

Photos: Stuart Cohen

The Evanston is the oldest courtyard apartment building in Evanston. With a picturesque exterior of flat brick surfaces and bay windows, it is one of only a few apartment buildings here that show the influence of the Prairie School. The wide uniform overhang of the hipped roof is a Prairie School trademark, as is the building's continuous stone string course at the sill of the third-floor windows reinforcing the building's horizontality. Terracotta trim in a pattern that combines geometric and naturalistic forms shows the influence of Frank Lloyd Wright's mentor, Louis Sullivan, the architect of the Auditorium Theater and the Carson, Pirie, Scott building in Chicago. The arched entryway in the courtyard is also Sullivanesque, and the planter urns on the porch in the courtyard are typical Prairie School features. Apartments vary in size from one to four bedrooms. SC

1014 Hinman Avenue

Architect unknown

1873

(Remodeled 1902 by Frank Lloyd Wright)

An oft-overlooked Wright design is this house remodeling for Dr. H.W. Hebert, Wright's dentist and uncle to John Howe, chief of the Usonian drafting room. Hebert bought existing houses and had them remodeled for others. Although modest, features of Wright's mature style can be seen in the low front porch with extended flat roofline and obscured entry; this compression of low space leading into higher open space within became typical of Wright's manipulation of spatial perception.

The home's upper story was destroyed by fire and rebuilt after Wright's death. The steep gables were original to 1873; the bank of gable windows were probably a Wright design as they echo Wright's Home and Studio and Moore House in Oak Park, and the Foster Cottage in Chicago. It is interesting to note that this project was undertaken in the same year as Wright's well known Dana House in Springfield and Heurtley Residence in Oak Park. **HH**

Church of All Souls

1407 Chicago Avenue
Architect: Marion Lucy Mahony
1904 (Demolished 1961)

The Church of All Souls was organized in 1891 by a group of Unitarian women who met for over a decade in Evanston homes. The first service was led by Rev. Jenkin Lloyd Jones, Frank Lloyd Wright's uncle. Marion Mahony's mother and aunt were members. The small stone chapel was Mahony's first independent work and the only building ever produced under her own name. In its Victorian neighborhood, the church had a strong presence with its elemental Gothic forms, triangular gable front and rough-hewn masonry walls. The simple rectangular auditorium, without an altar, lay under the open trusses of a timber-paneled roof. The tinted stucco interior was trimmed with oak panels, rails and planter brackets to articulate the form of the building's simple structural system. Mahony, Frank Lloyd Wright's first employee and principal delineator, was the world's first licensed female architect. She later became the wife and business partner of Walter Burley Griffin. JW

Perkins House (NR, LL)
2319 Lincoln Street
Architect: Dwight Perkins
1904

Noted architect Dwight Perkins employed many characteristics of the Craftsman style, along with rising Prairie School motifs developing in his offices at Chicago's Steinway Hall, in this house he designed for himself and his family. The stucco house has a high string course of wood strips with pairs of attenuated curved brackets dividing the upper story into six sections. The gabled roof extends its central peak over lateral rectilinear bays, while it hangs low over the front windows.

Additions to the west façade created a two-story lateral porch, now enclosed. The interior fireplace and decorative tiles were designed by Perkins and his wife Lucy Fitch, an accomplished artist and author. As the founder of the Cook County Forest Preserve system, Perkins valued the natural environment. He asked his friend and landscape architect Jens Jensen to design the extensive yard. It was shared with the house next door, designed by Perkins for his wife's sister.
KH

Brown House (LL)
2420 Harrison Street
Architect: Frank Lloyd Wright
1905

Photo: Jack Lesshafft

This modest home brings many of Wright's recurring elements harmoniously together. Most distinctive is the 22' wide by 9' deep cantilevered roof over the ground-level veranda. This horizontal line is further emphasized by thick-thin wood batten cladding extending into and narrowing the second floor. Typical of Wright, both the veranda and the small second floor porch are carved out of the mass of the house rather than added to it. Note the second floor's dark wood trim against white stucco, another favored feature. Inside the home are leaded interior windows and a Roman brick fireplace. Foreshadowing Wright's interest in affordable housing and city planning, documents indicate the Brown House may have been designed as a "tract" house: one of several similar houses to be built on a single tract of land. This house originally occupied its current and the adjacent corner lot. It was designed contemporaneously with Unity Temple (1904) and The Rookery (1905). **HH**

University Building (LL)
1604 Chicago Avenue
Architect: George Maher
1906

Photos (above): Jack Weiss
(below): georgemaher.com

This two-story mixed-use building has stores on the ground floor and office space above. The building is faced with limestone and its second floor has large "Chicago Windows," a central fixed window with double hung operable windows on either side. On Davis Street, the windows are set back and the length of the building is divided into thirds by two-story-tall columns. The columns' tops are pure invention and their flower motif is repeated in other locations.

The building's architect, George Maher, wrote about his "motif rhythm theory," the repetition of a floral design at different locations and in varying sizes. Each façade is surrounded by a decorative stone frame. Notice the treatment of the building's corners, where the vertical legs of this frame step in and then back out again. This is referred to as a "re-entrant corner," a feature of modern design that can be seen in the Chase Bank down the street. SC

Linthicum House (LL, DE)
1315 Forest Avenue
Architect: Tallmadge & Watson
1907

Photo: James Brannigan

An early and accomplished iteration of the Prairie School, the design of this house effortlessly combines many of the motifs and elements of the style into a composed statement. The simplified massing of buff Roman brick is capped with limestone coursing and a recessed, geometrically patterned cornice. References to architect Louis Sullivan's work are seen in the centralized arch of the roofline and the impressive arch of the porte-cochere. The three rectangular window openings on the second floor are divided by wide decorative mullions while all the windows have delicately styled art glass. A deep shed-roofed porch runs the length of the front façade established by substantial brick piers. The corner piers are larger with geometric limestone accents and surmounted by flattened stone urns. Tallmadge grew up in this neighborhood and lived all his life in this city. He designed many more houses, churches and the signature streetlights of Evanston. **KH**

Evanston Public Library

1703 Orrington Avenue
Architects: Charles A. Phillips and
James Gamble Rogers
1908 (Demolished 1960)

Photos: (above) Evanston Photographic Service
(below) Evanston History Center

Evanston's first library was located on the second floor of Old City Hall, but when the collection outgrew the space a library building was planned on land acquired from Northwestern University. The Library Board hired Charles A. Phillips and Games Gamble Rogers, who would go on to national prominence as designers of university buildings in the Gothic style. Almost half the funds for the new library were donated by Andrew Carnegie, the philanthropist remembered today for funding the Carnegie Libraries built in towns throughout the country. The new library was a Classical Revival building, a civic style popularized by the Classicism of Chicago's 1893 World's Columbian Exposition. Built of buff-colored Bedford limestone, the building had an Ionic portico. The interior was finished in mahogany with a 25-foot-high main lobby that contained the circulation desk. Evanston's first library building was demolished in 1960. SC

Kretsinger House (NR, LL)
1000 Forest Avenue
Architect: Tallmadge & Watson
1908

Tallmadge & Watson, best known as Prairie School architects, designed this house for William Kretsinger, founder and owner of the American Fork and Hoe Company. Among the numerous half-timbered houses in Evanston, the Kretsinger house best demonstrates the many stylistic influences on the Prairie School and on Chicago's progressive residential architecture. In addition to Tudor Revival and the English Arts & Crafts movement, this house shows the influence of Jugendstil, the German Arts & Crafts movement, and the Viennese Secessionists. Notice the decorative use of half-timbering on the gable ends grouping together windows, the tops of which follow the angle of the gable, a Prairie School feature. (See Tallmadge & Watson's house at 1136 Lake Shore Blvd.). The hipped end of the gable and the decorative timber squares are Jugendstil, while the porches with their brick corner piers and planter urns are distinctly Prairie School. SC

Patten Gymnasium
Northwestern University
2145 Sheridan Road
Architect: George Maher
1908 (Demolished)

Photos: (above) Western Architect
(below) University Archives, Northwestern Architecture

The Patten Gymnasium was a gift of Northwestern Trustee James Patten and was built in 1908 to replace a gymnasium building that had been constructed on the same site in 1876. The new gym's roof structure was of steel arched trusses, which were expressed on the building's curved Bedford limestone front façade. The building's sides were clad in pressed white face brick.

The building housed a gymnasium, an indoor baseball diamond and a ten-lane running track. The North Shore Music Festival was held in the main part of the gymnasium the year that the facility opened. In 1940 Northwestern University razed this gymnasium to make way for their Technological Institute. SC

The Parker Apartments

1635-41 Hinman/418-20 Church
Architect: William Barfield
1909

Commissioned by Dr. Andrew Parker for the site of his former house, this triad of six-flats was viewed as an asset to the city. The three-story building was constructed in the plan of an H, creating front and rear-facing courtyards. Barfield had designed several apartment buildings and a hospital in Chicago and a house in Evanston. The Tudor styling of this brick building is evidenced in the third story of half-timbering and stucco, along with oriels and the heavy stone Tudor arches of the main entrances.

Green marble, red quarry tile and dark oak in the entries enhance the motif. The apartments had oak wainscoting, built-in buffets and beamed ceilings. Visual interest is added to the hipped roof by the central forward and side gables. The balance and understatement of this extensive building, with its expansive front setback, create a harmonious interaction with the landscape of this prominent corner lot.
KH

Carter House (NR, LL, PA)
1024 Judson Avenue
Architect: Walter Burley Griffin
1910

Considered a masterpiece of Griffin's repertoire, this famous house was designed for a close friend of his sister's, Elsie P. J. Carter, and her husband, Frederick. The visual impression of the dominant central gable is enhanced by the horizontality of the projecting lateral eaves. The thin Roman brick of the first story rises into flanking piers, accentuated by narrow limestone caps. The wide timbering of the horizontal trim is reiterated with narrow wood strips defining the stucco surface of the projecting gable. Vertical counterpoints delineate the banded windows and rise to the peak of the overhanging eave. The elongated lateral porch that wraps the dining room extension was once open, expressing the transitional space between outdoors and in. Another hallmark, the obscured entry door, leads to a low hall. The impressive living room is anchored by a massive brick fireplace and inglenook. This quintessential Prairie School design is a superb apotheosis of the genre. **KH**

First United Methodist Church (NR, LL, DE)
516 Church Street
Architect: Thomas Tallmadge
1911

This venerable English Gothic Revival church was the third structure built for the pioneering Evanston Methodist congregation, founded in 1854. Church Street is named for the proximity of this institution, whose first wooden church (1856) was located at its intersection with Orrington Avenue. Congregant and native son Thomas Tallmadge, later of Tallmadge and Watson, designed this monumental limestone church on an orientation similar to the previous 1870 building by Cass Chapman. The imposing bell tower enhances the church's prominence on the site. Tallmadge designed the chapel and south additions in 1930 with the assistance of Ralph Adams Cram, who also created the oak reredos. James Hogan of London designed the stained glass windows, including one of Frances Willard, another notable member of the church. The structure is considered an important work of Tallmadge, also known for his Prairie School houses and Evanston's iconic streetlights. KH

The Judson (NR, LL)
1243–49 Judson/326–28 Dempster
Architect: Francis M. Barton
1911

Photos: (above) Stuart Cohen
(below) Granacki Historic Consultants

Amid Evanston's stock of vintage Tudor and Georgian apartment buildings, the austere Judson defies stylistic categorization. Its most pronounced architectural elements, the three entrances—two on Judson and one on Dempster—are also its most unusual feature. The splayed columns of the building's entry portals overlay the banded brick of the first floor. This is capped by a stone sill that runs around the building as a string course defining the building's base. On Judson, four sun porches with brick piers at their corners project forward of the main block of the building, enclosing the space of the ground floor entry vestibules. Just above the vestibules, the first-floor porch windows, painted black, project over the roof of the vestibules as a rectangular bay. This unusual "proto-modern" feature suggests that these windows define a volume of space that has been slipped between the brick piers. SC

Orrington School (LL)
2636 Orrington Avenue
Architect: Raeder, Coffin & Crocker
1911

Photos: (above) Jack Weiss
(below) James Brannigan

As the settlement of northeast Evanston increased after the turn of the century, this school was built to serve the expanding population on the site of a former cow pasture. Located on Orrington Avenue, the school and the street were named for Northwestern University founder Orrington Lunt. Evanston resident Henry Raeder designed the building in a simplified modern style, incorporating understated Classical ornamentation in the colonnaded entrance loggia with its red terracotta surround. Two stories of stucco walls rise over a raised red brick basement and are framed at the corners and entrance by engaged piers topped with sculptures of banded orbs and eagles poised for flight. In 1931, Evanston resident Frank Childs of Childs & Smith designed the northern addition in a slightly more elaborate Classical style. Foliated Corinthian columns and soaring arched windows define this section, which houses the gymnasium and auditorium. **KH**

Comstock House (NR, LL)
1416 Church Street
Architect: Walter Burley Griffin
1912

One of two adjacent houses designed by Griffin for Hurd Comstock, whose grandfather had owned several properties in the area, this significant Prairie School house is often cited as one of Griffin's best. Both houses were to be rental properties planned to share a garden and garage. Marion Mahony Griffin did the presentation drawings. Designed on a tri-level plan, the stucco and wood trim house is anchored by substantial concrete piers at the corners. The understated entrance is situated under a projecting second-story bay. The trapezoidal form created by the peaked gable with its wide overhanging eave is repeated in the soaring gable of the western wing. This striking studio space is set on a discrete level. The wide window muntins in geometric patterns, a hallmark of Griffin's style, are repeated throughout the interiors as well. The dynamic use of interrelated spaces creates a dramatic work of art. The second house of the pair has been remodeled. **KH**

Second Baptist Church (LL)
1717 Benson Avenue
Architect: Charles P. Rawson
1912

Second Baptist Church is one of two prominent African-American churches founded in Evanston in the 1800s. Prior to the earliest documented gatherings, prayer meetings may have been held in the late 1870s or early 1880s in the homes of Second Baptist's founding families such as Daniel F. and Mary E. Garnett. On November 15, 1882, ten of the African-American members of First Baptist Church (now Lake Street Church) requested and were granted letters of dismissal. On November 25, 1882, the Second Baptist Church was established with twenty members. In 1912, Reverend I. A. Thomas was installed as pastor and work began on the current building, which was dedicated on December 12, 1915. Rev. Thomas initiated a capital campaign in 1920 that later allowed the church to pay off its mortgage, build the parsonage and purchase its pipe organ. **JW**

Warren House (NR, LL)
2829 Sheridan Place
Architect: William Carbys Zimmerman
1912

Photo: Jack Weiss

This Tudor Revival house is one of Evanston's grand lakefront mansions with its limestone exterior, turrets, crenellations, decorative stone grotesques and carved floral patterns. Tudor arches, used on the exterior, repeat on the interior. The house's main stair has oak newel posts that are carved with a "three oaks" motif, a reference to the Warrens' hometown in Michigan. Edward Kirk Warren was a successful manufacturer whose company, the Warren Featherbone Company, made dress stays from turkey wing feathers rather than whalebone. The Warrens built their Evanston home on lakefront property purchased by Edward's wife, Mary Chamberlain Warren, from Northwestern University. Architect William Carbys Zimmerman is best known as the designer of the Illinois State Penitentiary in Joliet, although he continued to design houses throughout his career. SC

First Church of Christ, Scientist (DE)
(now The Music Institute of Chicago)
1490 Chicago Avenue
Architect: Solon Beman
1913
(Restoration 2003 by Otis Koglin Wilson)

Photos: (above) Stuart Cohen
(below) OKW

The First Church of Christ, Scientist was the fourth church to be built on Raymond Park. It replaced a remodeled frame house that had served the same congregation and is constructed of brick and Bedford limestone with a Classical entry porch. Solon Beman is best remembered as the architect of Chicago's Fine Arts Building and of Pullman, the neighborhood on Chicago's south side built by George Pullman for his railroad car employees. The former church's Classical exterior and magnificent interior were probably influenced by the classicism of Chicago's 1893 World's Columbian Exposition. Now used as a concert hall by the Music Institute of Chicago after its restoration by Otis Koglin Wilson in 2003, it contains one of the most beautiful Classical interiors in the entire Chicago area. In the main hall, its ribbed vaulted ceiling is cut into by clerestory windows along both sides that flood the top of the space with natural light. SC

Oakton School (NR, LL)
436 Ridge Avenue
Architect: Perkins, Fellows & Hamilton
1913

Design of schools was the primary focus of Dwight Perkins' office and Oakton School was typical of their designs. The cost of the 1913 building was $90,000. It is one of nine local landmarks in the Oakton Historic District and is home to nine Works Progress Administration (WPA) art pieces. The central corridor contains three carved pine bas reliefs by Alfred Lenzi installed in 1937: "Animals," "Wild Animals" and "Farm Animals". All three carvings are wonderful examples of Lenzi's talent.

A series of murals in the auditorium by Carl Scheffler and Ethel Spears depicting the legend of Charlemagne were recently restored. Evanston resident Carl Scheffler received his art education at Smith Academy and the Art Institute of Chicago. He was an art supervisor in the Evanston Public Schools and established the Evanston Academy of Fine Arts in the Carlson Building that he operated for 18 years. He also created the fairy-tale murals that decorate Haven School. **JW**

Skinner House (NR, LL)
208 Hamilton Street
Architect: Chatten and Hammond
1913

Built at the corner of Michigan and Hamilton opposite the Jernegan and Anthony houses, the Skinner house completes a fine ensemble of historic houses in Evanston. Edward Skinner was the manager of Wilson Brothers, a wholesaler of men's furnishings. The house combines many features of the progressive residential architecture of its day: Prairie School horizontality and an overhanging hipped roof, Arts and Crafts features such as long rows of casement windows and shutters with decorative cutouts and the skillful combination of Classical columns with an overall informality. The house was clearly influenced by the later work of Howard Van Doren Shaw, one of the Chicago area's most respected residential architects. The way in which the roof dormers are grouped to emphasize the entry and the center of the Hamilton façade and the blue-green color of the windows and exterior trim are features of Shaw's Lake Forest houses. SC

The Woman's Club of Evanston (LL, PA)

1702 Chicago Avenue
Architect: Ernest A. Mayo
1913

The Woman's Club of Evanston was designed by Ernest A. Mayo, a prominent Evanston architect and resident who designed 38 houses here. Mayo was an English-trained architect who practiced in South Africa before he came to Chicago to work on the 1893 World's Columbian Exposition. The Woman's Club was designed to look like a large red brick Georgian home. Its most prominent feature is the porch with two-story classical columns facing south. The club was founded by Elizabeth Boynton Harbert (1845–1925) to promote the "physical, social, mental, moral and spiritual development of its members." The club met in Harbert's home, and then in a variety of locations, until the current site was purchased in 1910. The club raised the funds for their building over the next three years with Northwestern University Trustee James Patten donating one-third of the building's cost. SC

Emerson Street YMCA

1014–16 Emerson Street
Architect: Shattuck & Hussey
1914 (Demolished 1980)

Known as "Emerson Y," this 1914 building served the African-American community for over 50 years. Beginning in 1909, supervised activities for children were held in a lot off Emerson Street as African-American youth were forbidden to join the main YMCA. Seeking a permanent home, business and religious leaders raised funds for the new $23,000 brick building. The Emerson Y offered a place for youth to learn sports and for organizations to hold meetings and banquets. Services included counseling, classes and camping trips. A performance by Nat King Cole was staged. In a 15-year effort to desegregate, the Emerson Y was closed in 1969. Failing to preserve the building, it was demolished in 1980. The documentary film *Unforgettable* was made to celebrate its history and public art installations on Emerson Street, Maple and Oak Avenues and University Place commemorate this place with images that illustrate the community icon that once was the Emerson Y. **LS**

Harris Hall (LL, PA)
Northwestern University
1881 Sheridan Road
Architect: Shepley, Rutan & Coolidge
1914
(Restoration 2009 by Weese Langley Weese)

Harris Hall, built as a home for the social sciences, was designed by Charles Coolidge, a principal of Shepley, Rutan & Coolidge, the architecture firm responsible for the Chicago Public Library (now the Chicago Cultural Center) and the Art Institute of Chicago. The Neoclassic building features colossal Ionic columns and decorative applied pilasters at the top story. Dedicated in 1915, Harris Hall was named in honor of Norman Wait Harris, a prominent Chicago banker and Northwestern trustee. After the building's completion the original classrooms and offices remained largely unchanged until 2009 when the university initiated a major restoration project. Weese Langley Weese designed the restoration and additions to the west and south, including a new monumental main entry stair. This LEED Gold building now serves as the home of the university's History Department and general-use classrooms. JW

640 Lincoln Street (NR, LL)
(formerly Roycemore School)
Architect: Lawrence Buck with
Tallmadge & Watson
1915–1927
(Library addition 1937 by Earl Reed)

Photos: Heidrun Hoppe

Roycemore School was built when the Evanston Academy–descendent of the 1871 Evanston College for Ladies–closed its doors. Roycemore's founders wanted their building to "have a maximum of light and air... preserve a home atmosphere...and avoid the...institutional appearance of the ordinary school building." The school achieved all of these ideals and remains virtually unchanged today. A rambling yet cohesive structure in the English vernacular style, the building has an axial formality around a central courtyard, flanked by slender wings with an informal, picturesque quality. Irregular massing, fenestration and rooflines all contribute to this effect. On the interior, single-loaded corridors allow an abundance of light; stairwells feature art glass windows and built-in benches for students to gather in conversation. The tragic 1918 influenza epidemic claimed Roycemore's first principal, Julia S. Henry, who died after only two years at her post. **HH**

Sears Modern Home "The Osborn"
2421 Simpson Street
Architect unknown
1915–1929

Photo: (above) Sears Roebuck Catalog of Houses, 1926
(below) Jack Weiss

Census data indicates that Evanston's population increased by 70% between 1920 and 1930. This intersects neatly with the heyday of the Sears Modern Homes program and the developing community of northwest Evanston. Six confirmed Sears mail-order homes were built here, and another 20-plus match catalog models but are to date unverified. Nearly all survive. Sears Modern Homes were produced from 1908-1940, with 447 different designs, by anonymous architects, following popular house trends of their time. A Sears home included everything needed for construction–precut, numbered and fitted–as well as plans and instructions. Innovations such as gypsum wallboard, asphalt shingles, central heating and electrical wiring were included or offered as they arose. Homebuyers could request modifications to materials and layout or even submit original blueprints and receive all materials ready for construction. *See Appendix E for a list of Evanston's mail-order homes.* **HH**

Swigert House (LL)
747 Sheridan Road
Architect: Howard Van Doren Shaw
1915

President of the Swigert Paper Company, Harry A. Swigert was also in the lumber business. Architect Howard Van Doren Shaw was one of America's best known residential architects. *Architectural Record* magazine wrote, "Mr. Shaw's houses...are charming and inviting to a degree rarely exceeded in American domestic architecture–a fact which justifies Mr. Shaw's success as well as accounts for it." Shaw was so highly esteemed by his colleagues that he was awarded the American Institute of Architect's Gold Medal. It would be easy to dismiss the Swigert house as just another brick Georgian, until one notices how the symmetry of the Sheridan Road façade is broken by the location of the door and by the tall window at the stair landing. Here we can see Shaw's work transforming the domestic architecture of his day through his extraordinary and unexpected sense of composition. SC

Rapp House (LL)
2733 Colfax Street
Architect: Robert Seyfarth
1916

This elegantly simple house was designed for Earl Rapp and sold a few years later to Thomas Hunter, a LaSalle Street bond trader. It was the first house on the block across from what is now a forest preserve. Robert Seyfarth was one of the North Shore's most prolific residential architects. He had worked for George Maher supervising the construction of Maher's Evanston work. This early house has some of the features of Seyfarth's later work: a simple volume with gable ends facing the sides, regularly spaced windows with shutters and abundant light from floor-to-ceiling windows on the ground floor. Seyfarth admired Howard Van Doren Shaw, and this house's stucco finish and arched windows may have been influenced by the house designed by Shaw at 2233 Orrington Street (1909). Although this house doesn't appear on any list of Seyfarth houses, the building permit at the Evanston History Center's Research Room identifies Seyfarth as the architect. SC

Shakespeare Garden (NR, LL)
Northwestern University
2121 Sheridan Road
Landscape Architect: Jens Jensen
1916
(Dedicated 1930)

Henry IV, Falstaff:
"For though the camomile, the more it is
trodden on the faster it grows, yet youth,
the more it is wasted the sooner it wears."

Photo: University Archives, Northwestern Architecture

A former trash dump is the site of landscape architect Jens Jensen's garden tribute to William Shakespeare. Shakespeare often found metaphors in nature for the human condition, and so the Drama League of America chose a garden as a suitable memorial for the 300th anniversary of the bard's death. The Garden Club of Evanston was key in siting, funding and construction of the tribute. Jensen, a member of the Drama League, is known for his affinity for natural prairie landscapes rather than historic Tudor garden traditions. He resolved this by imagining the garden as "a sun-opening in the woods" with a formal center and woodland border. Shakespeare mentions many plants in his plays, but they were found to be too spreading in habit or not hardy in this climate. Plants selected were, however, common to Elizabethan England. The sundial and fountain are not original to Jensen's design; the fountain was designed by Daniel Burnham's son, Hubert Burnham. **HH**

73

Dryden House (NR, LL)
1314 Ridge Avenue
Architect: George Maher
1917

George Maher, usually considered a Prairie School architect like Frank Lloyd Wright, designed this Georgian Revival mansion for George B. Dryden, a rubber manufacturer, and his wife Ellen, niece of film manufacturer George Eastman (of Eastman Kodak). Mrs. Dryden wanted a home that looked like her uncle's 50-room mansion in Rochester, NY, especially given that Mr. Eastman provided the money to build the house. Mr. Dryden served on the Board of Trustees of Northwestern University along with James Patten, for whom Maher had designed a far more unconventional stone house at 1426 Ridge. One hint in the Dryden home of Maher's penchant for reinventing the vocabulary of architecture is the design of the two-story entry portico columns. These have transformed Corinthian capitals with an Egyptian look similar to those on the Maher-designed bank in Winona, MN. The Drydens' property had plantings by the famous Midwestern landscape architect Jens Jensen. SC

Johnson House

2614 Lincolnwood Drive
Architect: Frank Lloyd Wright
1917

Photos: (above) Courtesy Anne Mosio Hanney &
Suzanne Hanney; (below) thefranklloydwrighttour.com

Despite the many homes he designed for wealthy clients, Wright always had an interest in well-designed, affordable housing. This came to fruition with his American System-Built Homes: like Sears kits, materials were shipped pre-cut to the site. The difference lay in that Arthur L. Richards owned the exclusive right to develop the homes with Wright's designs. Of the 25 constructed, 15 survive. Evanston's Johnson House is one of these unusual Wright creations. Economical and compact in size, the house is similar in massing to Wright's Unity Temple rather than his more well-known Prairie Style. Although renovations have eliminated the slab chimney and much of the trim, one distinct element remains: the mass of the stairwell on the south is pulled away and visually separated from the rest of the building by thin strips of glass. The project ended when materials became unavailable due to WWI. Wright subsequently sued Richards for royalties and fees. **HH**

75

Trow House (NR, LL)
1000 Sheridan Road
Architect: Mayo and Mayo
1919

Designed for banker John F. Trow, this Cottage Style house is atypical of Ernest Mayo's work. He was best known for his numerous and highly popular half-timbered Tudor Revival houses built along Forest Avenue (1120, 1203, 1210, 1318) and Sheridan Rd. (1117, 1218, 1225). The Trow house, on a corner lot, has its entry on Lee Street with an all-glass sun porch facing east. Its columns are unusual because the profile at the top and bottom are the same. In contrast to the house's white painted stucco walls, the entry door is surrounded by red brick quoining, a feature of the English Arts & Crafts houses of M.H. Baillie Scott. The house's most distinctive feature is the rounded edge of the roof. Cedar shingles were soaked in water for several days and then bent to form this curve in imitation of a thatched roof. SC

Evanston Pumping Station (LL)
1455 Elmwood Avenue
Architect: F. L. Barrett
1920

This unique municipal building with Prairie School features is built of red brick with limestone detailing. By the mid-1920s, Evanston was a mature city with paved streets, an excellent fresh water filtration plant—the only one on the lake—and an extensive sewer system. Evanston was acknowledged to be ahead of other lake towns in sanitation facilities. The sewage pumping station on Elmwood, now a part of the Metropolitan Water Reclamation District system, was built at a cost of $506,000. At that time it pumped sewage from Evanston's lakefront into a 10-foot sewer on Lake Street, discharging it into the North Shore Channel. Today the sewage is pumped to the water reclamation plant at Howard Street and McCormick Boulevard. The 600-acre area served by the pumping station is bounded by the lakefront, Evanston's south border, Ridge Avenue and Emerson Street. There are six centrifugal pumps in the building. JW

Thayer Cottages
2303–2321 Thayer Street
Architect: R.B. Williamson
1920

Photos: Heidrun Hoppe

A particularly charming group of houses lines the northeast end of Thayer Street. These single-story homes were part of the expansion of population into northwest Evanston during the period following World War I. All were constructed at the same time by builder J.A. Ross for owner J.H. Kraemer & Son. The wood frame houses, set well back from the street, resemble country cottages more than city residences and feature simple gable roofs and small enclosed entry porches.

Pine trees surrounding the homes enhance the perception of being in a woodland setting. Two basic features– the direction of the roof ridge and whether or not the entry porch features a gabled roof or a shed roof–vary house by house. Some of the buildings have been demolished or altered over the years to be nearly unrecognizable and now interrupt the formerly consistent rhythm of roof and porch; six retain their original design. **HH**

1122 Harvard Terrace
Architect: George Klewer
1922

Photo: Jack Weiss

There are 45 Craftsman style homes in the Oakton Historic District. The house at 1122 Harvard Terrace was designed by George Klewer. Klewer designed 19 Craftsman residences in the District and a total of 40 overall. The architects who worked throughout the District were not the highly visible society architects of the time. Rather, they were a group of men catering to the upper middle class of the 1920s, clients who wanted quality of both design and craftsmanship without having to obtain these in the purchase of a Sears kit house. Features of the Craftsman style include the expression of the house's construction. The Craftsman house typically has exposed rafter ends and roof beams or triangular knee braces set under gables. The roofs are most often gabled, but sometimes hipped, and usually low-pitched. JW

McGuire House (NR, LL)
1140 Lake Shore Boulevard
Architect: Harwood Hewitt
1925

This Tudor Revival house was designed by Harwood Hewitt of California for Thomas D. McGuire, a real estate broker. The local architect was Herbert Riddle. Five years after the house was completed, McGuire's daughter, Martha, married Herbert Riddle. The house is faced in a decorative brick pattern called Flemish Cross Bond, with cut stone around the entrance and at the house's corners. The roof is slate and the steel casement windows are painted blue-green to match the patina of the house's copper work. A story-and-a-half high bay window in the living room overlooks the lake. The living room is on the second floor, is two stories high and runs the full depth of the house. From the entry hall a stair ascends half a story to this space, which is situated over the garage. Large windows face east and west, and French balconies on either side of the fireplace face north. SC

First Congregational Church (LL)
1445 Hinman Avenue
Architect: Tallmadge & Watson
1926

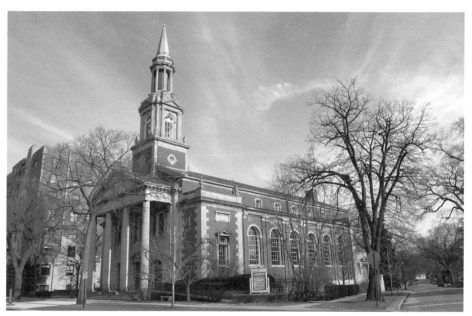

At the east end of Raymond Park, the First Congregational Church's Classical portico and tall steeple dominate this park, which is reminiscent of a New England town green. The current structure is built on the site of the church's original building, constructed in 1886. This Colonial Revival Church, done in the Classical style, recalls the work of the 17th century English architect Sir Christopher Wren. The American influence of Wren's work may be seen in the buildings of the College of William and Mary in Virginia. The church's architects, Tallmadge & Watson, are best remembered as Prairie School architects, but were capable of designing Classical architecture based on Thomas Tallmadge's knowledge as an architectural historian and author. While many of their Prairie houses still remain, Tallmadge once wrote that he lived to see all but a handful of his commercial commissions torn down to make way for new construction. SC

Ridgeway Bungalows
2301–2319 Ridgeway Avenue
Architect: M. Fishman
1926

Photos: (above) Heidrun Hoppe
(below) Jack Weiss

Although Evanston has a tradition of diverse and distinctive homes, there are a few instances where one owner built several nearly identical houses. When the houses are well-designed and placed, the rhythm they create on the street becomes a very pleasing unity. The six small brick bungalows on Ridgeway are such a grouping. Two designs, which differ only modestly, alternate down the block. Each one-story home is set well back from the street and features three full height arched colonial windows on the main façade. Crisply delineated side walls end in a gable that rises slightly above the pitched roof. Although the houses appear quite tiny, when built each contained 6 rooms (including 3 bedrooms and a bath, plus a "ping-pong room" in the basement) for a cost of $11,000. The building permit further states the exact amount of building materials per home: 75 square yards of plaster and 25,000 bricks. **HH**

The Varsity Theater
1710 Sherman Avenue
Architect: John E.O. Pridmore
1926

The Varsity Theater was one of the largest movie palaces ever built in suburban Chicago, boasting 2,500 seats. It was also one of the most spectacular, styled like a 16th century French chateau, with a ceiling designed to look like a nighttime sky with twinkling stars and floating clouds in its ceiling. No expense was spared on luxury by its original owner, Clyde Elliot, an Evanston native who had worked in Hollywood for many years. From marble imported from Italy to antique tapestries, the Varsity rivaled many of neighboring Chicago's finest theaters. The theater was absorbed into the Balaban & Katz chain a decade after its opening. Over the years the Varsity changed hands several times but remained a popular fixture of downtown Evanston until it closed in 1984 and was converted to mixed-used retail. JW

Carlson Building (LL)
632–40 Church/1633–49 Orrington
Architect: Stanley M. Peterson
1927

This is the fourth structure built in Evanston by local developer Victor Carlson. The first was Library Plaza, followed by the Orrington Hotel and the John Evans Apartments. The Carlson building was intended to complement the adjacent Library Plaza, which was also designed by Stanley M. Peterson. Created to house offices of the city's doctors, it has long served this purpose. The Carlson's vertical, Neo-Gothic design was reinforced by dark green spandrels that have since lightened, lessening the effect. The central tower was to have been seven stories higher than the rest of the building, but was reduced by the zoning commission. The entrance is marked by two-story arched windows. The Art Deco bronze interior detailing also graces the doors of the elevators, which were run for many years by two beloved elevator operators, whose retirement and obsolescence were sorely lamented. A later annex received the first Evanston Art Commission award in 1928. **KH**

The Chaumont (NR, LL)
531 Grove/1501–11 Chicago
Architect: Thielbar & Fugard
1927

Photo: (above) southeastevanston.org
(below) Jack Weiss

The Chateau de Chaumont is an elegant commercial/residential building that carefully integrates retail shops on the first floor with private apartments on the three floors above. Inspired by the detailing, materials and layout of the chateaux of central France, the exterior is of honed Bedford Stone with a slate Mansard roof that hides the building's fourth (and top) story. A hidden inner courtyard, also typical of historic chateaux, is built on the roof of the shops below and provides private entries for the apartments. The distinctive chimneys attest to the wood-burning fireplaces originally provided in every apartment. By turning its retail face to Chicago Avenue and its private entry to Raymond Park, the Chaumont creates a transition between business and residential spaces in downtown Evanston. This division is further manifested in the large retail windows on the first floor which contrast with the multi-paned veil of the apartment windows above. **HH**

Clark House (LL)
(now Evanston Art Center)
2603 Sheridan Road
Architect: Richard Powers
1927

Photos: Courtesy of Evanston Art Center

The Harley Lyman Clark house was built on lakefront property purchased from the Deering family of International Harvester. Clark was president of the Utilities Power and Light Company and his house was the last large residence to be constructed in Evanston before the stock market crash. The architect, Richard Powers, relocated to Chicago from Boston. The design of the house seems equally inspired by French Norman and English Cotswold architecture, with its randomly coursed masonry walls, carved limestone and red sandstone trim and red Ludovici tile roof. With its multiple roof lines, many chimneys and dormers, the house is one of Evanston's most picturesque mansions. Within, the rooms were arranged to provide views all the way through the house in both directions. This provided a view of Lake Michigan from the front door. In 1949 the building was sold to Sigma Chi Fraternity and in 1963 it became the Evanston Art Center. SC

Lake Shore Apartments (NR, LL)
470–498 Sheridan Road
Architect: Roy France
1927

Located at the bend in Sheridan Road where it becomes South Boulevard, the Lake Shore Apartments offer Evanston's best views of Lake Michigan. The east-facing façade sets back in steps and gently swelling bays to maximize views. The top floor, a story and a half high, has breathtakingly tall windows. The nearly block-long building has multiple entryways including a courtyard entered from South Boulevard. French Renaissance in style, this brick building is unusual because what looks like cut stone–the entire ground floor, classical pediments, window surrounds, pilasters, rosettes and urns–is glazed terracotta. Terracotta is a molded, manufactured clay product which is glazed and fired. Chicago's landmark skyscraper, the Reliance Building (1895), was the first building to make extensive use of this product. Clad entirely in terracotta, it was derided in the press as "A Washable Monument." SC

Michigan & Lee Apartments (NR, LL)
940-950 Michigan Avenue
Architect: Frank W. Cauley
1927

*Photos: (above) Stuart Cohen
(below) Thshriver, Wikimedia Commons*

Courtyard apartment buildings line the streets of Chicago and Evanston with their courtyards, opening to the street, typically facing either east or west. The apartment building at the corner of Michigan Avenue and Lee Street, built in 1927 and designed by Frank W. Cauley, is an interesting variant. Its courtyard is entered diagonally from the street corner where the building is set back to create an automobile drop-off and turnaround. The building's two street façades end in curving bays that round the space of the street into the courtyard. Within each apartment unit, the living and dining rooms are marked on the building's exterior by glass doors with wrought iron railings. The sunken courtyard of this elegant brick and limestone Georgian Revival building is also a distinguishing feature. Here, tiers of glass French doors stack above recessed entry porches with Classical columns, creating a courtyard whose walls are almost all glass. SC

The Rookwood (NR, LL)
718–734 Noyes Street
Architect: Connor & O'Connor
1927

Photos: (above) Jack Weiss
(below) Thshriver, Wikimedia Commons

The Rookwood, designed toward the end of the era of great Evanston apartment houses, is spare looking in comparison to earlier Evanston apartment buildings. With simplified Tudor-style details and large steel sash windows, the limestone entryways and stone courtyard walls are the building's dominant design features. The courtyard walls are made of random ashlar limestone. These form gateposts surmounted by lanterns marking the entries to the two courtyard spaces.

The building is three stories tall above an English basement, and contains 51 apartments ranging in size from studios to three bedrooms. What is unique about the building is the design and use of open landscaped spaces. These open off Noyes Street and provide access to the building's multiple entryways. The easternmost landscaped space runs back from the street the full depth of the building. It has a paved terrace, perimeter walkways with park benches and a large central lawn. SC

Selling House (LL)
900 Edgemere Court
Architect: Mayo & Mayo
1927

Ernest Mayo and his son, Peter, featured this house prominently in monographs of their work. Modeled after English country houses, it is built of red brick with minimal limestone accents. It has a strong axial plan with the living room set at a central cross axis. Its vaulted ceiling is nearly three stories high, with a balcony overlooking it from the second floor hallway and a window to the third floor ballroom. The gabled east façade consists of an impressive composition of leaded glass windows. Arched limestone porches flank the north and south façades. The basement boasted a pool, with fireplace and grotto, and a gymnasium. The first floor includes a paneled library, "Mah Jong" room of inlaid jade and quartz and wrought iron gates at the dining room entrance. For many years the house was the home of billionaire Henry Crown, whose philanthropic donations in Evanston resulted in buildings named for his children Robert and Rebecca. **KH**

Zecher House (LL)
1006 Harvard Terrace
Architect: Dewey & Pavlovich
1927

Photo: Jack Weiss

This Chicago Bungalow is one of the more notable bungalows in the Oakton Historic District which includes 20 other Chicago bungalows and 45 Craftsman bungalows among the 141 single-family homes. The presence of architect-designed work in the design of the houses in the district is self-evident. Though the architectural styles vary throughout the district, the quality of design rarely does. Architects who designed these houses specified brick as the construction medium and the roofs were virtually all concrete tile. Throughout the houses, high quality interior trim, doors and windows were called out in the specifications. Fireplaces were design features that highlighted the abilities of master masons and they regularly appear in brick, cobblestone and tile. In addition to the single-family homes in the district there are also entire streets of two-flats in similar architectural styles utilizing the same construction methods. **JW**

Nichols School (LL)
800 Greenleaf Street
Architect: Childs & Smith
1928

It is fitting that the design of the school named for longtime School Superintendent Frederick Nichols reflects his commitment to the arts in education. The central section is modeled after the Doge's Palace in Venice, the iconic example of the Venetian Gothic style, with its two stories of wide, pointed arches and upper row of oculus windows. The 75-foot clock tower reflects the similarly adjacent St. Mark's campanile in the Piazza San Marco. Generously proportioned windows in the flanking wings are further representations of this style. Dedicated to progressive education and integrating art in learning, Nichols personally donated an extensive art collection to Evanston schools and encouraged installation of New Deal art. The school's interior was enhanced with many murals, tapestries and Nichols' mosaic tile works, which he created in his studio in the school basement. Architect Frank Childs was a native Evanstonian. **KH**

Chandler's Building (LL, DE)

630 Davis Street
Architect: Edgar Ovet Blake
1929
(Renovation 1999 by Holabird & Root)

Photo: Jack Weiss

Chandler's originally occupied three buildings on the busy downtown corner of Davis and Orrington. Henry Chandler's store offered books and supplies to Northwestern students and also sold sporting goods, typewriters and office furniture. It handled event tickets, offered art classes and sold Crosley cars from a catalog. Actor John Malkovich was Chandler's most famous employee. When the current building owners renovated the property in 1999, they demolished the three-story corner building and created an open plaza with landscaping and outdoor seating. The plaza, enclosed on two sides by the remaining buildings, has a protected feeling and is a center of calm in a busy area. The remaining L-shaped structure was renovated in concrete with Indiana limestone cladding and Tudor-style windows. It includes street front retail and offices with abundant natural light; the top floor features loft-like offices with 15-foot ceilings. LS

Colonnade Apartments (NR, LL)
501–07 Main/904–08 Hinman
Architect: Thielbar & Fugard
1929

Photos: *Chicago Architectural Annual*

The Colonnade Apartments, at the northwest corner of Main and Hinman, was named for its second-floor colonnaded loggia overlooking Main Street. Built in 1929, the Classical limestone and brick building resembles an Italian Renaissance Palazzo. Designed by the Chicago architectural firm of Thielbar & Fugard, its plan is unique. While apartment buildings with retail shops incorporated into their ground floor are not unusual in cities, the Colonnade Apartments are a brilliant variant on this idea. The apartment building is entered from Hinman Avenue through a wood paneled, Tudor-style lobby. From there a stair ascends to a second-floor landing where a glass door opens to a covered loggia surrounding all four sides of an open courtyard. Here each side of the apartment building has its own exterior entrance to a stair that serves two apartments per floor, with the apartments overlooking either the street or the courtyard. SC

Evanston YMCA

(now McGaw YMCA)
1000 Grove Street
Architect: Chester Howe Walcott
1929

The YMCA occupied several downtown Evanston buildings since its founding in 1885. In 1898 the Y moved into its own new building at 1611–21 Orrington designed by Holabird and Roche. In 1925 the YMCA hired Chester Walcott to design a new limestone-clad, Gothic-inspired building at 1000 Grove Street. The larger facility included a 172-room residence for men, two gymnasiums, a swimming pool and other amenities. In 1969 the Emerson YMCA, which had served Evanston's African-American community since 1909, merged with the Grove Street facility. A major expansion in 1984 included the addition of a larger gym and second swimming pool. Walcott was a graduate of Princeton University and studied architecture in Europe. Walcott designed a number of North Shore residences, churches, country clubs and schools. He is best known for his St. Chrysostom's Episcopal Church in Chicago. JW

95

Marshall Field & Company (LL)
(now Evanston Galleria)
1700 Sherman Avenue
Architect: Graham Anderson Probst & White
1929

The Marshall Field building, a smaller replica of the flagship store in downtown Chicago, was constructed in 1929 for $850,000 and was one of Fields' first suburban locations. A combination of French Mansard and Art Deco styles, the building's stone exterior includes ornamental green bronze trim at the canopies, spandrels, flagpoles, lights and other fixtures. The clock, also made of green bronze, is a replica of the clock at the Chicago store. A variety of openings include large ground level display windows, large windows organizing the middle floors and dormer windows penetrating the Mansard roof. The main shopping floor is taller while the top floors are shorter to accommodate offices. The store closed in 1987 after nearly 60 years and was completely renovated for retail, commercial and residential use. The exterior clock was restored to working order; bronze and brass finishes were refurbished and interior renovation included marble and trim restoration. **LS**

National College of Education
2840 Sheridan Road
Architect unknown
1930 (Demolished 2007)

National College of Education began in 1886 as a college to train women as kindergarten teachers. Founder Elizabeth Harrison believed that the future prosperity of a community began with the education of its youngest children. She also believed that teaching was a noble and difficult profession that demanded a college degree. Harrison's groundbreaking work helped launch the National Parent-Teacher Association and the Head Start program. NCE became the first college in Illinois to offer a four-year teaching degree. The Evanston campus, established in 1926, was sited on four acres on the border of Evanston and Wilmette. In 1990 National College of Education was renamed National Louis University. In July 2006 the University relocated its programs to their Old Orchard Campus. Today, only Baker Demonstration School, a laboratory school once associated with National College, remains adjacent to the site. JW

South Boulevard CTA Station (LL)
601 South Boulevard
Architect: Arthur U. Gerber
1931

A survey of Evanston's built environment would not be complete without referencing the visual impact of the Chicago Transit Authority's raised commuter line (the Purple Line) through the center of the city. The South Boulevard station typifies many of the structures related to the Purple Line. This station, built in 1930–31, replaced the Calvary Cemetery station one block south. This site was far better suited to serve the increasing population in new apartments being built in Evanston. Designed by Arthur U. Gerber, who also designed the very similar Sheridan station on Chicago's Red Line, the South Boulevard station combines elements of Doric and Beaux Arts designs, executed in terracotta. Trademark Gerber details include the laurel-framed cartouches, pair of Greek Revival Doric columns, globe lights and the words "Rapid Transit" above the door in terracotta. JW

Deering Memorial Library (LL)
Northwestern University
1935 Sheridan Road
Architect: James Gamble Rogers
1932

*Photos: (above) Evanston History Center
(below) University Archives, Northwestern Architecture*

Facing west to a great lawn, Deering Library was intended to be the center of the campus. It was constructed with funds from the estate of Charles F. Deering and from the McCormick family, whose companies formed International Harvester. With the construction of a new library in 1970, the Deering Library now houses the university's collection of fine art books, maps, special collections and university archives. The building's main reading room is a stunning two-story- high space with an exposed timber ceiling. The library was supposedly modeled after the King's College Chapel (1515) in Cambridge, England. The architect, James Gamble Rogers, trained in Chicago in the office of Burnham & Root and was related to the McCormick family by marriage. Rogers, who moved his practice to New York, is best known for his buildings at Yale University. His work popularized the architectural style that became known as "Collegiate Gothic." SC

Dauber House (LL)
2769 Asbury/1234 Isabella
Architect: Frank Polito
1934

Photo: Jack Weiss

The property at the southeast corner of Asbury and Isabella consists of four parcels of land. In 1934 Frank Polito designed a two-story, two-family Art Deco dwelling and a single-story brick garage for Carl Dauber. The white brick cornice, banded in black, the entry portals and the porthole windows above are typical of Art Deco houses across the country. In 1980 the owners at the time, who had purchased the house in 1972, were granted a zoning variation to add a two-story addition to the rear of the existing garage. The addition created a third dwelling unit and two more parking spaces. In the late 1930s and early 40s other Art Deco homes and a townhouse were built on Wesley Avenue in south Evanston and at 3545 Golf Road near Central Park Avenue. JW

Freeman House (LL)
2418 Lincoln Street
Architect: Robert Seyfarth
1935

While Seyfarth's contemporaries designed houses in various styles, Seyfarth's houses usually employed non-specific traditional residential elements in just a few simple compositional arrangements. He designed a number of houses, like the Freeman residence, with either two or three front-facing gables of brick or buff-colored stone. On all his masonry houses, he used decoratively carved limestone lintels or arched surrounds to give importance to the entrance.

The front of the Freeman house is virtually identical to the Mayfield house in Glencoe, built at the corner of Montgomery and Sheridan roads in 1926. Both have an interesting play of asymmetrically arranged windows. The Freeman house should be compared to the R.A. Page house just to the north at 2424 Lincoln, which has a carved lintel above the doorway and dormer windows set into the roof, a signature feature of many of Seyfarth's houses. SC

Mullins House (LL)
3200 Harrison Street
(originally 2501 Central Park)
Architect: Bertrand Goldberg
1936-1937

Photos: (above) Hedrich Blessing
(below) Heidrun Hoppe

This wood-frame, wood-clad house is only the second building designed by Bertrand Goldberg. Starkly simple on the street face, the living/dining areas and upstairs bedrooms open to an intimate rear courtyard with awning windows extending all the way to the ceiling line. During this time Goldberg was experimenting with modern rectilinear forms and had not moved into the sculptural curvilinear work we associate with him in Chicago (Marina City, Prentice Women's Hospital, River City). Still, in 1936 the house was considered so unusual–and such a threat to property values–that newspapers reported the "Affair Mullins," an attempt by neighbors and elected officials to either change zoning laws to forbid the dwelling or purchase another site for the home. A suitable site was not found and City Council voted unanimously to allow construction. In two ironic twists, the house was moved in 1951 and was subsequently named an Evanston landmark. **HH**

328-342 Wesley Avenue (LL)
Builder: Fred Walsh Co.
1937

In September 1937 a building permit was issued to developer Fred Walsh Co. for the construction of an 8-unit tan brick townhome in the Art Deco style. Walsh, a long-time resident of Joliet, Illinois, established a real estate business there and later turned to development. This townhouse is unique in Evanston for its impressive scale. Art Deco emerged after World War I when rapid industrialization was transforming culture. One of its major attributes was an embrace of technology. Deco flourished during the 1930s and 40s, then waned in the post-World War II era. Deco architecture, like the art, interior furnishings and products of the time, responded to the demands of the machine, new materials and the requirements of mass production. This block of Wesley features several other Art Deco single-family homes built in the late 30s and early 40s. Another large single-family Art Deco home can be seen at 3545 Golf Road in Skokie/Evanston. **JW**

United States Post Office (LL)
1101–05 Davis Street
Architect: John C. Bollenbacher
1937

Photos: (above) Heidrun Hoppe
(below) Mark2400, Flickriver

During the Depression, Franklin Roosevelt's New Deal built over 1,100 post offices throughout America. A Public Works Administration report from 1939 stressed the need for high quality design to ensure "public works of an enduring character and lasting benefits." Our Main Post Office is one of these buildings. Its massive but simple design of honed limestone suggests strength and permanence, perhaps to instill faith that we would overcome the difficulties of the Depression. Inside the tall public space, polished marble walls alternate with louvers and 18-foot-high windows. The terrazzo floor is laid out in a geometric pattern echoed in the design of the ceiling above. Brass and stone writing desks, each with its notice board and light, create a repeating rhythm along the south wall. All is reflective of the "Machine Age" sensibility of hard-edged machined metal and stone. "New Deal Art in Evanston" describes the four sculptures that are also a part of this beautiful building. **HH**

Will House (LL)
2949 Harrison Street
Architect: Perkins Wheeler & Will
1937

Architect Philip Will, Jr., designed this home for himself and his family. An extremely modern design in 1937, it received much attention and won several awards. Of all his work, Will was said to have been the most proud of this house. His purpose was to create a split-level house for an informal lifestyle. He chose heartwood cypress for the horizontal board and batten siding. Bearing some resemblance to Wright's Robie House in its elongated massing on a narrow corner lot, Will once referred to its lines as those of an ore boat on the Great Lakes. The steel casement windows are banded and grouped at the corners. The second-story family room opens to a roof deck. There are two bedrooms on the second floor, with the master bedroom and combination living and dining room on the first floor. Will lived here until 1980, a few years before his death. **KH**

Milburn Park (NR)
2, 4, 6-12 Milburn Park
Architect: Raymond Houlihan,
1937 -1939 and 1946
(later houses facing the lake by John
Normille, 1954 and Cohen & Hacker,
2013)

Photos: Stuart Cohen

Located at the end of Milburn Street, on the east side of Sheridan Road, the houses surrounding Milburn Park were built by developer Charles Hemphill. Hemphill built eight lannon stone houses with slate roofs in English Tudor Revival and Colonial Revival styles. All the houses have their formal entrances located off a common lawn with attached garages accessed from the streets on the north and south sides of the development except for the three houses facing the lake.

Two of the lakefront houses were built at later dates, including one which has recently been torn down. Milburn Park is bounded on the north by the Grosse Point Lighthouse and on the south by Northwestern University. The stone used for the Hemphill houses is the same stone used on many of Northwestern's buildings along Sheridan Road. This provides a subtle sense of visual continuity between the university and these adjacent houses. SC

The Cradle (LL, DE)
2049 Ridge Avenue
Architect: Schmidt Garden & Erickson
1939

Founded in 1923 by Florence Dahl Walrath, the Cradle continues a legacy of adoption throughout the world. The Evanston Landmark building, a 58,000-square-foot, Gothic style stone structure, stands prominently on the corner of Ridge and Simpson. A dormitory wing was added in the 1950s to house the Infant Nursing School students. In 2001, an extensive renovation including landscape and signage was accomplished. Outdoor seating, nestled among trees and plantings, provides a contemplative greenscape. Unique among adoption agencies, the Cradle is the only adoption agency in the country with an on-site nursery and is a leader in infant care practices and methods, with development early-on of sterilization methods that saved many children's lives. When the building was completed in 1939, a mechanical barrier to kill airborne germs was designed and a germicidal light that destroyed germs was also installed. **LS**

2940 Harrison Street (LL)
Architect: Perkins Wheeler & Will
1940

Lawrence Perkins designed this house for speculation. Across the street from his partner Philip Will, Jr.'s house, Perkin's house also sits on a narrow end lot. With end gables and engaged chimneys it has a southern early Colonial reference. Its modern fenestration is distinguished by the small, evenly spaced upper story windows, while the first floor is punctuated by rows of individual square glass block windows. The brick walls of the entrance portico are perforated with similar square openings. The attached garage creates an enclosed private yard and patio. The house was built a few years after Will's house, at the same time as their collaboration with Eero and Eliel Saarinen on the seminal Crow Island School in Winnetka. The school marks a turning point in the development of the young architectural firm, which went on to become one of the largest and most successful in the field of educational architecture. **KH**

Scott Hall (NR, LL)
Northwestern University
601 University Place
Architect: James Gamble Rogers
1940

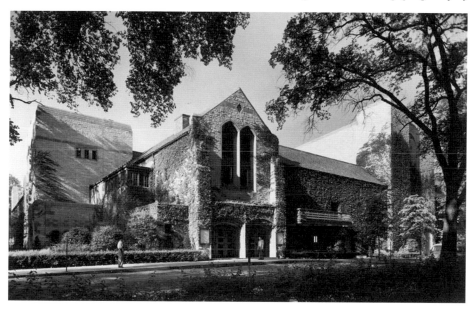

Scott Hall was designed to address a pressing need for a building to house the activities of the campus women's groups and to center the social, intellectual and artistic life of the campus. It was the original home of the Amazingrace Café. Fundraising began in 1915 at the initiative of students. In 1938 Walter Dill Scott announced his impending retirement as president of Northwestern University. A committee decided that a new student center bearing his name would best memorialize Scott's contributions to the University and the community. The modified Gothic, T-shaped structure of gray lannon stone was designed by James Gamble Rogers to complement his Women's Quadrangle to the west and his Deering Library to the east. In keeping with the intention of Scott Hall's planners to make it a cultural center, Cahn Auditorium, seating over 1,200, was built on its north side. Scott Hall was remodeled in 1973 and Cahn Auditorium underwent a major renovation in 1995. JW

Clark House (LL)
333 Wesley Avenue
Architect: Wilson Connell, Jr.
1941

Nestled on a block-long section of Wesley Avenue that hosts several other Art Deco homes, this two-story brick veneer single-family house typifies the style made popular in the 30s and 40s. Most development in south Evanston had come to a halt with the stock market crash of 1929. Construction of single-family bungalows and large, multifamily apartments east of Asbury ended. In the late 1930s and early 40s home building resumed west of Asbury.

On Wesley and further west, a variety of smaller houses in a range of newer styles, from Neo-Colonial to Raised Ranch, were built. There are other examples of Art Deco in north Evanston, including the double house at 2769 Asbury. This home at 333 Wesley is typical of Art Deco in its crisp, white forms and flat roof. A one-story frame family room was added to the rear of the house in 1964. JW

Newby-Ennis House (LL)
200 Dempster Street
Architect: William DeKnadel
1941

This home on the former Daniel Burnham estate merges aspects of the Prairie School with a more contemporary form. The term Contemporary has been used to classify a style dating from the 1940s that incorporates some of the tenets of modernism, but often with a less rectangular form and occasionally with a little ornamental trim. The multi-level flat roofs at 200 Dempster have cantilevered eaves. The first floor is brick with a recessed entry while the second floor has wide wood siding and Prairie-style ribbon windows. DeKnadel had worked as an architect under Frank Lloyd Wright at Taliesin in Spring Green, Wisconsin, from 1932–1933. In 1937 he designed "Windway," the house for plumbing manufacturer Walter J. Kohler, Jr., in Sheboygan, Wisconsin. In 1941, and again in 1957, DeKnadel was the lead architect on successful committees to save Robie House, the Frank Lloyd Wright masterpiece in Chicago, from demolition. JW

Technological Institute (DE)
Northwestern University
2145 Sheridan Road
Architect: Holabird & Root
1942
(Renovation 1999 by Skidmore, Owings
& Merrill)

Photos: (above) Northwestern University
(below) University Archives, Northwestern Architecture

"Tech", the main building for the Robert R. McCormick School of Engineering and Applied Science, has over 750,000 square feet of teaching and research labs, classrooms and offices and is one of the largest academic buildings in the world. Construction began in 1939 and was funded with a $34 million gift from a railroad equipment inventor who wanted to provide a "cooperative school that was second to none" with academic courses and practical hands-on experience. It is built of lannon stone and Bedford limestone in the shape of two E's, back to back and joined by a central spine. Entrances are marked with bas-relief sculpture by Edgar Miller depicting science and engineering themes. Two new wings were constructed in 1961 and a new entrance terrace in 1973. The 10-year renovation completed in 1999 reconfigured the interior and upgraded building systems. Recent renovations were made to the entrance terrace off Sheridan Road. LS

Merrick Rose Garden (LL)
Lake Street and Oak Avenue
Landscape Architect: Ralph Melin
1948

Photos: (above) walkscore.com
(below) Rachel Goldberg, Evanston Patch

The Merrick Rose Garden was designed as a tribute to Clinton Merrick, Alderman of the 2nd Ward for 23 years. The focal point of the tranquil, bi-level garden is the cast-iron Centennial Fountain. In 1912 this fountain replaced the deteriorating original fountain at Fountain Square, which had been installed in 1876 to commemorate 100 years since the signing of the Declaration of Independence. The replica was removed from Fountain Square in 1946. It was restored and rededicated at the Merrick Rose Garden on July 4, 1951. A garden wall built in 1987 carries history in its recycled bricks from Evanston's old brick streets. The Merrick is a test site for All-American Rose Selections, Inc., a group of hybridizers and growers developing new roses. One year before they are available for retail sale, new varieties are donated and planted here for display. In 2004 the Merrick Rose Garden showcased 2,000 roses of approximately 200 varieties. **HH**

Main Street Houses
1616-1708 Main/847 Dewey
Architect: G.E. Watts
1949

A housing boom following World War II hit Evanston in the 1940s and 50s, using up most of Evanston's remaining vacant land and filling a need for affordable "starter" homes for returning veterans and new families. These one-story brick houses are typical in their modest size (under 1,000 square feet) and low-slung simple design featuring new trends such as picture windows. Developed by Charm House Builders of Evanston, the unusual feature of these houses is in their thoughtful layout on the site.

Rather than individual homes lined up facing the street, these eight houses are arranged as two groups of four around central courtyards, which simultaneously fits more buildings on the lot and lends the feeling of expansive open space. The south houses are mirror images of each other; the western house in each group has a modified corner entry. Each house has a private back yard and garage; a ninth house sits alone facing Dewey Street. **HH**

Christian Science Reading Room
1936 Central Street
Architect: Michaelson, Rabig and Ramp
1954

Photos: (above) facebook.com
(below) Heidrun Hoppe

In 1879 Mary Baker Eddy founded the Church of Christ, Scientist. In 1888, to encourage reading of her seminal work *Science and Health with Key to the Scriptures*, the first Christian Science Reading Room was established in Boston. Today there are over 1,200 reading rooms, each unique to its location. Evanston's Reading Room follows this tradition. Sited on a corner lot formerly occupied by a gas station, the Reading Room was designed to open to the corner, to two streets and to a private rear garden, expressing both its public and private face on a busy street. Materials such as brick, glass block, granite, sandstone and clear and opaque glass are integrated in this tiny building. C.S. Michaelson was a former partner in the firm Michaelson and Ragnstad, designers of Chicago's Garfield Park Fieldhouse and the Pui Tak Center in Chinatown (formerly the On Leong Merchant's Association Building), both built in 1928 and both Chicago Landmarks. **HH**

Unitarian Church of Evanston

1330 Ridge Avenue
Architect: Schweikher, Elting & Bennett
1958

Located on 1-1/2 acres of land purchased in 1954, once the estate of Irving Osborne, the Unitarian Church replaced an earlier structure built on the site and was designed to accommodate growth. Build of pre-cast reinforced concrete and completed in 1958, it was the first building in Evanston to use the tilt-up construction process. Five side-wall "bents" provide bracing for both the walls and the roof. Between the bents are pre-cast slabs perforated by long, narrow windows of slag glass. The north and south walls of the building contain 1,750 sq. ft. of tinted glass. The church received awards from the Chicago Association of Commerce and Industry and the Chicago Chapter of the American Institute of Architects for its "outstanding contribution in the fields of architectural design, craftsmanship and construction." JW

580 Ingleside Park
Builder: Schurecht, Inc.
1961
(Addition 2000)

In 1959 Dr. Edwin Reinholtzen, DDS, wanted to construct a brick veneer, single-family home with a detached two-car garage on Lot 7, a large 75-foot by 142.5-foot parcel in the private Ingleside Park north of the Grosse Point Lighthouse. He hired Schurecht, Inc., a Chicago builder, to design and build the modern house. In May 1958 Schurecht had designed a home in Barrington Hills for a former Evanston resident, Edward Ford, whom Dr. Reinholtzen probably knew. Classified as Contemporary–a style dating from the 1940s–the design features naturalistic touches seen in Prairie and Craftsman homes and features broad, overhanging eaves. It moves away from the more severe and rectangular Modernist style. In 2000 then-owner Dr. Ira Salafsky contacted architect Jerry Hamen to design a second floor addition. Set back 33 feet from the front, the newer open glass area appropriately complements the original first floor façade. JW

117

Atlas House
647 Sheridan Square
Architect: Keck & Keck
1961

Photos: Trulia.com

George Fred Keck was an early designer of modern and passive solar homes. This elegant single-story residence, fronted by a brick wall and opening onto a private courtyard, contains many of the distinctive Keck and Keck features: flat roof, indirect lighting and passive solar heating through large fixed thermopane windows with separate operable vents. Keck brought modernism to popular attention as architect of the House of Tomorrow and the Crystal House for Chicago's 1933–34 Century of Progress Exposition. In 1937 he helped create the New Bauhaus, a school modeled on the original Bauhaus of Weimar, Germany. Under director Lazlo Moholy-Nagy and mentor Walter Gropius (director of the original Bauhaus), the New Bauhaus brought in such luminaries to teach as Alvar Aalto, Buckminster Fuller, Richard Neutra and Man Ray. It later became the Institute of Design at the Illinois Institute of Technology. William Keck joined his brother as manager in 1946. **HH**

Alice Millar Chapel & Religious Center

Northwestern University
1870 Sheridan Road
Architect: Jensen & Halstead
1964

This 700-seat Neo-Gothic chapel with Modern touches is a highly visible landmark standing where Chicago Avenue terminates at Sheridan Road on the south end of Northwestern's campus. The Foster G. McGaw family donated this chapel in honor of Mr. McGaw's mother, Alice. The massive front window of stained glass is illuminated from within, making the building a night-time beacon to motorists and pedestrians alike. The interior is spatially grand and comparatively modern.

There is no lavish Gothic ornament here as there is in James Gamble Rogers' Neo-Gothic Deering Library or Scott Hall, designed in the 1930s and 40s. Touches of Modernism can be seen in the strips of faceted stained glass in the lobby wall. The chapel contains twelve large stained glass windows; the entire south wall is stained glass from top to bottom. All were designed and painted by Belgian-born designer Benoit Gilsoul and fabricated by Willet Studios in Pittsburgh. **JW**

119

Calumet & Hecla Office Building
(now Baha'i National Center)
1233 Central Street
Architect: Bertram A. Weber
1964

This '60s Modern structure, originally the Calumet and Hecla Office Building, is currently headquarters for the Baha'i Community in the United States. The Baha'i faith, best known in this area for the Baha'i House of Worship in Wilmette, was founded in Iran in 1844 and introduced to the United States at the World's Columbian Exposition in 1893. Bertram Weber, born in Evanston in 1898, is the second of three generations of Chicago architects. He graduated from MIT in 1922 and worked briefly for Howard Van Doren Shaw. Weber's prolific career centered on picturesque homes on the North Shore but also followed emerging trends. Weber's assured design includes slender arched columns creating a grand entry space, bands of windows accentuated by flat "eyebrows" and the style's typical balance between delineated forms and flat, unadorned massing. The second floor extends to create a porte cochère supported by a broad triangular column.
HH

Haid House
1221 Michigan Avenue
Architect: David Haid
1968

Photo: One Hundred Years of Chicago Architecture

The houses architects design for themselves frequently serve as either advertisements for their work or experimental laboratories. David Haid's elegantly refined one-story house is neither; it is an expression of belief in the ideas of his teacher Mies van der Rohe. This brick, steel and glass house has four bedrooms and an open plan living and dining room skillfully arranged on this narrow lot. The living room has a floor-to-ceiling glass wall overlooking the front yard. Privacy for the bedrooms, which also have floor-to-ceiling glass, is provided by one-story tall brick walls which form courtyard spaces. While courtyard houses have been around for millennia, modern versions with walls of glass that visually connect inside and outside date from Mies van der Rohe's demonstration house at the 1931 Berlin Building Exposition. Haid's best known structure is certainly the glass garage pavilion in Highland Park which stars in the movie, "Ferris Bueller's Day Off." SC

Rebecca Crown Center
Northwestern University
633 Clark Street
Architect: Skidmore, Owings and Merrill
1968

The Rebecca Crown Center was the gift of Henry Crown and his sons in honor of their wife and mother, who died in 1943. With a 100-foot-tall clock tower as its focal point, it is an icon for Evanston. Designed by Walter Netsch of Skidmore, Owings & Merrill, the limestone and concrete building and plaza contains Northwestern University's central administrative offices. The building is designed in the Brutalist style, with repetitive, angled geometries. Concrete walls with limestone slabs act as sun visors for tall windows. The City closed a portion of Orrington Avenue and rerouted traffic to accommodate the three-building complex and expansive plaza that comprises 2.7 acres in downtown Evanston. Netsch designed seven buildings on campus and his architectural style has set the tone for subsequent buildings for the university. LS

State National Bank Plaza (DE)
(now Chase Bank)
1601 Orrington Avenue
Architect: Shipporeit-Heinrich Associates
1969

Evanston's first skyscraper, the 22-story former State National Bank building, owes its form and its plaza to Chicago architect Mies van der Rohe's iconic Seagram Building in New York City. The Seagram Building (1958) literally created a new image for corporate America and convinced city planners of the virtues of urban plazas as adjuncts to tall office towers. The Bank's plaza is the site of an elegant round glass banking pavilion. The round form emphasizes its importance and unlike the one-story post office building in Chicago's Federal Center plaza, which defines the edge of a space, the banking pavilion sits in the larger space of the plaza, street, and Fountain Square. The architect, George Shipporeit, worked for Mies van der Rohe and today is best known as the architect of Chicago's cloverleaf glass apartment building, Lake Point Tower, also inspired by an early Mies project. SC

DeCoster House
17 Martha Lane
Architect: Keck & Keck
1973

This modest house was built for Northwestern University professor Cyrus DeCoster, who was the author of eleven books on 19th century Spanish literature. The residence's nationally known architect, George Fred Keck, was one of Chicago's early pioneers of modern architecture. Keck's Crystal House, built for Chicago's 1933–34 Century of Progress Exposition, was a revolutionary all-glass house with a steel structure of exposed exterior roof trusses and exterior truss columns. Keck was an early pioneer of passive solar houses who also explored prefabrication. This house, done late in his career, has many signature features typical of his houses from the 1940s on: flat roofs, vertical wood siding and natural stone work. Most notable are the large fixed windows flanked by louvered ventilating panels. These had screens and hinged solid panels that opened inward to admit fresh air. He designed many houses on the North Shore including 647 Sheridan Square in Evanston. SC

Wilson House
529 Judson Avenue
Architect: Hinds Schroeder Whittaker
1973

Photo: *(above) Architectural Review*
(below) Stuart Cohen

The design of the Sea Ranch Condominiums in California, by the firm MLTW, with weathered siding and single pitched roofs recalling vernacular sheds and barns, changed residential architecture in America in the late 1960s and early 1970s. Richard Whittaker, the "W" in MLTW, was head of the Department of Architecture at the University of Illinois, Chicago, when Charles Wilson came there from Yale University to teach sculpture. The Wilson house has a single pitched roof typical of the Sea Ranch idiom, with the main living rooms on the second floor opening to the south to a roof terrace. The house has angled interior walls with all of the living spaces open to one another. This skillfully designed Contemporary house is one of only a few in southeast Evanston. SC

Pick-Staiger Concert Hall
Northwestern University
50 Arts Circle Drive
Architect: Loebl Schlossman Dart & Hackl
1975

"When you go to a performance, you go to listen to the music," observed Edward Dart, Pick-Staiger Concert Hall's lead designer. "But at the same time it is a visual experience." The visual allure of Pick-Staiger begins as you approach the building: its gleaming white façade floats before a sweeping lakefront panorama that culminates to the south with the dramatic view of Chicago's skyline. As you come closer, your eyes catch the jewel-like shimmer of the glass-fronted lobby. Dart's nod to the interplay of senses continues as you walk into the main hall. From the lower level, only about half of the hall's 1,003 seats are visible, yet the presence of a substantial balcony is barely evident, making Pick-Staiger feel simultaneously spacious and intimate. The unobstructed sightlines focus naturally on the stage and the hall's muted earth tones fade into the background. JW

Robert Crown Center

1701 Main Street
Architect: O'Donnell Wickland Pigozzi
1975

The Robert Crown Community Center and Ice Complex provides a variety of community services for the City of Evanston. It was designed by an Evanston-based architectural firm, O'Donnell Wickland Pigozzi. The facility is a one-story masonry building containing 63,500 square feet and is set four feet below grade to minimize its scale in the residential neighborhood. The complex includes a large ice skating arena with seating for approximately 1,000 spectators, a small studio-practice rink, a basketball court/gymnasium, a pre-school room and a number of other program/multipurpose rooms as well as locker room facilities and outdoor playing fields. Shani Davis, who was the first black athlete from any nation to win a gold medal in an individual sport at the Winter Olympics, learned to speed skate with the Evanston Speed Skating Club at Robert Crown Center. Davis won both gold and silver at the 2006 and 2010 Winter Games. JW

First National Bank of Chicago
(now Chase Bank)
1900 Central Street
Architect: David Haid & Associates
1978

The design sensibility of Modernist architect David Haid is visible in the austere lines and simple form of this branch bank. On the exterior, a slender curtain wall is balanced by thin slabs of brick veneer and the restrained metal "cornice" representing the roof joists within. Unfortunately bank security prohibits a photograph of the delicate interior office mezzanine, hung from the structure with slim steel framing. Haid, a former apprentice cabinetmaker, moved from Canada to Chicago in 1951 to study with Mies van der Rohe at the Illinois Institute of Technology. He began working in Mies' architectural firm almost immediately and remained for 9 years. Haid entered popular culture when the private automobile pavilion he designed in Highland Park was featured in the 1989 film, "Ferris Bueller's Day Off." The pavilion was actually smashed by the Ferrari in the movie and was repaired under Haid's supervision. In 1968 Haid designed his Evanston home at 1221 Michigan Avenue. **HH**

Evanston Terraces (DE)
1201–1229 Central Street
Architect: Booth Hansen
1980

Photos: Hedrich Blessing Photographers

In this townhouse development 43 multistory, 16-foot-wide party wall houses fill the long narrow site. They are built on top of a parking garage from which each townhouse can be entered directly, a smart site planning alternative to providing each townhouse with its own separate garage. On top of the garage structure, two rows of townhouses and their main entrances face each other across a landscaped "mews." The townhouses are built of brick with simple stone trim. Exterior fireplace chimneys, pitched roofs, gently angled front walls, carefully arranged windows and recessed entryways differentiate the individual townhouses. The simple use of traditional residential elements identifies this development as an elegantly restrained example of the Postmodern style. SC

Evanston Public Works Service Center
2020 Asbury Avenue
Architects: Sisco/Lubotsky Associates
and Concoer/Morgan with Stuart Cohen
and Andrew Metter
1982

Photos: Barbara Karant

This 140,000-square-foot complex hosts Evanston's Forestry, Streets, Sanitation and Building Maintenance Departments plus an employee parking garage, vehicle storage and refueling and materials storage yard. It was designed by the Sisco/Lubotsky team, all long-time Evanston residents. The building is an example of Postmodern architecture that combines traditional and classical architectural forms with modern design. A bridge that connects to the parking structure at the east end of the complex forms a gateway and formal entrance to the storage yard and maintenance building to the west. The two gable roofs on the bridge above the entryway cap two caretaker's apartments on the second floor; using glass for the enclosures below visually extends the bridge's width. The incorporation of "buildings" on the bridge recalls the many industrial bridge and loading structures in the Chicago area. JW

Schipporeit House

1225 Asbury Avenue
Architect: George Schipporeit
1984

In 1973, George Schipporeit, who had his home and architecture office in Evanston, applied for a permit to construct a new home at 1225 Asbury. A 2-story, 6-room frame house built in 1908 previously stood on the site. Schipporeit, a professor at the Illinois Institute of Technology, had worked in the office of Mies van der Rohe and is well known for Lake Point Tower, the only major building in downtown Chicago located east of Lake Shore Drive. Construction on the new home stopped in 1975 and the building permit was cancelled in 1977. Financial issues were resolved and new permits were applied for. Construction of the 2.5-story, 4,800-square-foot reinforced concrete home resumed in 1982. The boldly rectilinear Modernist home is striking in the context of its Victorian neighbors. Schipporeit's professional offices were located in the State National Bank Plaza and One American Plaza, both Evanston buildings that he had designed. JW

840 Michigan Avenue
Architect: David Hovey/Optima
1985

Photos: Scott McDonald, Hedrich Blessing

As a developer and architect, David Hovey's residential projects significantly impacted multifamily housing in Evanston. His first Evanston project, these townhouses at the corner of Michigan and Main are two buildings separated by a courtyard. The buildings each contain 8 townhouses with their own walled private gardens and 4 penthouses with private roof terraces. The buildings sit atop an underground parking garage entered from a ramp on the west. All the units are accessed from the courtyard via stairs and bridges made of steel with aluminum gratings enclosed in translucent channel glass. These are sculptural elements in the courtyard and are painted bright yellow and blue in contrast to the dark green steel panels under the continuous horizontal windows. The buildings are built of brick bearing walls with precast concrete floors. Unabashedly modern, the low-key exteriors fit comfortably into this neighborhood of traditional buildings. SC

North Pointe

2555 Gross Point Road
Architect: David Hovey/Optima
1990

Photos: Jon Miller, Hedrich Blessing

North Pointe is the second Evanston project designed by David Hovey. A 118-unit multifamily residential development, it features a single four-story condominium structure and a grouping of three-story townhouses arranged around a small landscaped lake. What makes North Pointe unique among contemporary Evanston multifamily locations is this private interior space, reminiscent of many of the well-known Evanston courtyard apartment buildings, but brought into a modern aesthetic. As with other residential projects that preceded and followed North Pointe, Optima managed every phase of the project from concept and financing through design and construction. Hovey's graduate thesis at the Illinois Institute of Technology explored the possibilities of factory-built housing, concepts clearly visible in the tubular steel balconies, glass block walls, pre-cast concrete panels and cantilevered I-beam canopy over the condominium patio. JW

Evanston Public Library

1703 Orrington Avenue
Architect: Joseph Powell with Nagle Hartray Architecture
1994

In 1991 28-year-old architect Joseph Powell won the international design competition for Evanston's 115,000-square-foot library. The library references the Prairie School, recalling Frank Lloyd Wright's Larkin Building in Buffalo, NY, and conveys its civic prominence. Exterior vertical piers in iron spot brick are topped by decorative cast-stone Prairie elements. On the south plaza, benches, trees and a clock tower invite passersby. Upon entry, an open stair orients patrons as they move between floors. Three-and-a-half story windows stretch to a white pine vaulted ceiling. Steel plates cast into the support columns allow for future expansion. Public art pieces include Michele Oka Doner's "Book Leaves," Beverly Stucker Precious' "For Endless Trees" and Ralph Helmick and Stuart Schechter's "Ghost Writer," a 1,600-pound, 40-foot-long sculpture hung in the main stair. Outside, Richard Hunt's "Bookends" tops the piers along the library's south face. **LS**

Mary & Leigh Block Museum of Art (DE)
Northwestern University
40 Arts Circle Drive
Architect: Lohan Anderson Architects
2000

The nationally renowned Mary and Leigh Block Museum of Art moved to a permanent building on the Northwestern University campus to house its ever-growing collection. The new glass, steel and limestone museum tripled the size of the original building to 20,000 square feet. Dirk Lohan, grandson of architect Mies van der Rohe, was the building's designer. Housing more than 4,000 works of art including significant historical and contemporary prints, drawings, photographs, film, video, sculptures and mixed media works, the museum is surrounded by an outdoor sculpture garden and many arts-related buildings. The glass-enclosed central circulation stair presents a recognizable destination on Arts Circle Drive. The Pick-Laudati Auditorium is home to the University's film series, lectures, classes and symposia. The Print, Drawing and Photography Study Center provides a dedicated space for research and viewing. **LS**

Church Street Plaza

Church Street & Maple Avenue
Architect: ELS/Elbasani & Logan
2000–2003

Church Street Plaza, a 176,000-square-foot mixed-use project, opened to the public in phases starting in November 2000. Arthur Hill & Co. developed the project on land formerly owned by Northwestern University and the City of Evanston. It was the first and largest element of a successful effort to reinvent and revitalize downtown Evanston as a retail and entertainment destination west of the "traditional" downtown. An open semi-circular plaza at the corner of Church and Maple visually and literally connects the new development with the rest of the downtown district. On the corner opposite the curving plaza is the round glass corner of the former Border's building designed by Nagle Hartray Architecture. The Plaza is anchored by Century Theatres, which offers cinemas totaling 3,400 seats in 18 auditoriums. The Plaza hosts a variety of retailers and restaurants, a Hilton hotel, Optima Views–a 205-unit condominium designed by David Hovey/Optima–and a 1,400-car public parking garage. JW

Optima Towers (DE)
1580 Sherman Avenue
Architect: David Hovey/Optima
2001

Photos: Jon Miller, Hedrich Blessing

This 13-story exposed concrete apartment building sits on a prominent site across from Fountain Square. The ground floor contains shops and restaurants and follows the line of the street, with three floors of apartments above. Forming a base, these apartment floors set back to create private roof terraces. Above this, the building sets back again, in angled facets, to create partially inset balconies. The building is entered off Sherman Avenue through a courtyard space created against the side of the adjacent landmark brick building. The projecting balconies on the upper floors have perforated metal balcony railings painted orange. The color is a complement to the tower's green floor-to-ceiling glass and picks up on the red-orange brick of the adjacent building. In addition to 105 units and ground floor commercial space, Optima Towers has a gym, swimming pool, party room and a parking garage for its residents. SC

Peacock Lofts (DE)
2144 Ashland Avenue
Architect: John Leineweber & Mary F. McAuley
2001
(Original building, 1927; Architect: J.A. Schrening)

Photo: Susan G. Andrews, SGA Photography

Redevelopment adapted the former Peacock Ice Cream factory to comfortable live/work spaces for the 21st century. An ornamental gate, fabricated by Makai Metals, opens onto a walkway accented with iron sculptures, gargoyles, antique signage and plantings of Japanese maples. Seven unique loft units are situated side by side along the winding walk, each with its own private entry. Ranging in size from 900 to 2,000 square feet, the lofts are designed as large unobstructed spaces on the first level, open partially to the bow-truss roofline and triangulated skylights twenty feet above. Elegant spiral staircases access the mezzanine levels that provide one or two additional room areas and private south-facing decks. Peacock Lofts is one of ten loft developments—including Fanny's Lofts—developed by Leineweber and McAuley that have reconfigured old light manufacturing structures to form an informal "Arts District" near the heart of downtown Evanston. **JW**

Levy Senior Center (DE)
300 Dodge Avenue
Architect: Ross Barney Architects
2002

Photo: Steve Hall, Hedrich Blessing

Ross Barney Architects used materials that recall historical park structures to create a see-through, pavilion-like building in 27-acre Robert E. James Park. A showcase for natural lighting and passive solar control, a glass-enclosed classroom wing is shielded by a 13-foot-high louvered wood screen allowing views into the park. The multipurpose gymnasium/theater is constructed of light-transmitting fiberglass. Offices and support spaces are clad in brick and aluminum. Functional components of the building create a courtyard containing an enabling garden and outdoor classroom, providing additional program space. In addition to natural and park-like qualities, materials were selected for durability, accessibility and sustainability. A natural slate border around the courtyard arcade provides a tactile warning and high-contrast definition for users who are visually impaired. Sassafras wood louvers are a weather resistant, sustainably harvested species. **LS**

Fire Station No. 3 (DE)
1105 Central Street
Architect: Yas Architects
2004

This highly visible fire station, situated on the major east-west axis of Central Street, is adjacent to the Metropolitan Water Reclamation District canal and the Central Street CTA stop. Striking views upon approach show the red and tan square face brick that clads the private "house" functions of the station interior. The glass-enclosed main vehicle bay directs light into the station and provides passersby a glimpse of the function of the fire station within, while glowing as a beacon after dark. The emergency vehicles and a vibrant yellow roof truss are visible through the glass. A fire hose "folly" tower is clad in grey metal panels and set off by a yellow steel structure that supports the flagpole and announces the presence, strength and dignity of the fire service. LS

817 Hinman Avenue (DE)
Architect: Torvik Associates with David Fleener
2005

This six-story condominium building is located in southeast Evanston on a street dominated by multifamily housing in vintage buildings. The building's Contemporary design is composed of limestone, brick, large glass areas and metal panels. Containing two units per floor, the building is oriented east-west to maximize natural light and views. All units have generous balconies and the two penthouse units have two stories and rooftop patios. The building massing creates solids and voids that reduce the building's scale while allowing more opportunities for light and views. Soft-loft units–similar to industrial loft residences in their open floor plans–are also contained within the building. The first floor unit includes a landscaped front yard. Tall ceilings are sculpted to the underlying steel structure. LS

Ford Motor Company Engineering Design Center (DE)
Northwestern University
2133 Sheridan Road
Architect: Davis Brody Bond
2005

The six-story Engineering Design Center was Northwestern's first LEED Silver-certified facility. Measures to achieve this "green' status include: (1) Minimizing the building's impact on the surrounding environment: an integrated retention basin captures rainfall to irrigate the historic Shakespeare Garden and returns excess runoff directly to ground water rather than the city sewer system; (2) Enhancing the quality and safety of the interior environment: natural daylight is provided to over 75 percent of the building's interior spaces—a remarkable achievement considering that two of the six building floors are below grade; and (3) Incorporating innovative approaches to environmental sustainability: the building employs an automated solar tracking system to close window shades in the face of direct sunlight and open shades in areas away from the sun. Visitors entering the building have an open view directly into the engineering shop on the first lower level. JW

Sienna Court

1740 Oak Avenue
Architect: Roszak ADC
2007
(Site addition 2010 by Booth Hansen)

Sienna Court condominiums comprise two buildings of a four-building project planned around a large landscaped courtyard by Roszak ADC. The original building is noteworthy for its use of roof terraces and duplex townhouses entered from the street. These have individual entryways and front yards and form the base of the high-rise apartment above. Shortly after the completion of the second building, a collapse of the roof garden over the parking garage resulted in the project ending without being fully realized. In 2010 the architecture firm Booth Hansen received approval to complete the site with a 174-unit rental apartment building at 1717 Ridge Avenue on the west side of the site. The new building matches the glass and brick materials used by Roszak in the original Sienna buildings. JW

Jewish Reconstructionist Congregation (DE)
303 Dodge Avenue
Architect: Ross Barney Architects
2008

The "greenest" synagogue to date in North America, the JRC replaced its original building and is adjacent to a city park, community center, commuter train tracks and residences. The design balances the limitations of a small site with an ambitious program promoting worship, educational and community objectives. JRC's commitment to Tikkun Olam–Hebrew for "repairing the world"–is manifest in the construction of a sustainable building. On a modest budget with a holistic design approach, the synagogue achieved a LEED Platinum Certification. The form and the material of the building, a precious wooden box, is a visual testament to these values. The wood cladding is reclaimed cypress harvested from dismantled mushroom houses. The design uses the original building's demolition waste for engineered fill. Site trees that could not be saved were harvested for interior finishes. Local construction waste was placed in gabions and used as site retaining walls. LS

Metal House 2 (DE)
1216 Main Street
Architect: Berry/Spatz
2009

Photo: Andrew Spatz

Metal House 2 sits on a tree-lined street surrounded by single-family dwellings and Metal House 1, its predecessor by 25 years. The 50x140-foot lot has access from the street and a rear yard facing south. Living, dining and kitchen spaces are located in the rear of the property taking advantage of the southern exposure with a 20x23-foot window wall, allowing privacy and buffering street noise. The upper level contains three bedrooms and a master suite. The lower level contains a work studio, laundry and additional living space. This highly insulated, passive solar home includes cost-effective green building elements. An overhang on the upper floor accommodates needed space while allowing natural light to filter into main living spaces and the lower level studio. Controlled views take advantage of green lawns and trees. Natural ventilation promotes a healthy environment. Grey aluminum siding makes the home virtually maintenance free. **LS**

Clark Street Beach House (DE)
1801 Sheridan Road
Architect: David Woodhouse Architects
2010

Photo: Andy Tinucci/David Woodhouse Architects

The Clark Street Beach House forms a subtly designed and understated gateway connecting 11-acre Centennial Park to Evanston's lakefront. The exterior cladding is regional lannon stone salvaged from the nearby building it replaced. Other materials—ground-face concrete block, gently reflective, matte-silver metal—were chosen to blend the building into its beachfront surroundings. The angled roof plane echoes the lines of the neighboring trees, allowing natural light and ventilation through high-walled restrooms. Rainwater runoff is deposited on the new 30-foot-wide belt of dune grasses, mediating between the park's trees and lawns and the wide-open sandy beach. As the Midwestern seasons change, so does the building. Large metal shutters swing wide when the beach season opens, showing summery greens and yellows. In winter, shutters swing shut, showing grays and ochres. LS

Fire Station No. 5 (DE)
2830 Central Street
Architect: Muller + Muller
2010

Photo: Mark Ballogg

Fire Station No. 5 is a high-performance facility replacing the original station built in 1954. It is the City of Evanston's first LEED Gold Certified building and is situated on a tight urban site in a neighborhood commercial district. The building incorporates many environmentally sustainable features including natural light, renewable and recycled materials, high efficiency mechanical systems, a thermally efficient enclosure and storm water management/collection for washing trucks. Fifty percent of the electricity comes from purchased wind power. The two-story design with a three-truck bay allows returning fire trucks to pull through the rear alley, eliminating the need for hazardous reverse maneuvers on busy Central Street. The brick volume provides an anchor relating to older neighborhood buildings and gives a sense of permanence and privacy. Enclosed in glass apparatus bays, the fire trucks are on display as a show of openness and assurance. LS

Heuberger House (DE, PA)
1801 Wesley Avenue
Architect: Audrain Architecture
2010

Situated in the Ridge Historic District, this home occupies a sunny corner lot. The owners charged their architect with designing a crisp, contemporary residence. The neighborhood context consists of wrap-around porches, pitched roofs, large windows and masonry and stucco façades. The new home incorporates many of these contextual cues, but boldly asserts itself as a new, modern home. The primary entry faces Wesley, but the entrance steps and French doors opening to the porch relate the house to all directions. Glass-railed decks and balconies provide layers of light and reflection into and out of the home. The exterior is stucco and Indiana limestone. Broad expanses of glass to the south, west and east open the residence into the historic district, reflecting a contemporary feel but acknowledging a respect for its more traditional neighbors. LS

SHOP Studios (DE)
940 Pitner Street
Original architect unknown
c1950s
(Redevelopment 2010 by Berry/Spatz)

Located in the West Evanston Industrial District, the original building is a 1950s single story, blonde brick, bowstring truss building. The adaptive re-use/mixed-use conversion has five rental units ranging in size from 1,000 square feet to 1,400 square feet. Open interior space with enclosed areas for privacy is the highlight of these live-work studios. Daylighting and natural ventilation were important design goals. Sustainable strategies include glass block on the south wall with additional new glass on exterior walls, fixed and operable skylights, and a 3'-6" wide storefront door with an operable transom to allow fresh air movement. An exterior gated walkway provides secure access from the parking lot. New aluminum exterior siding and "screens" are virtually maintenance free. The studios are attractive for offices, artist studios, and other local businesses. LS

Lehman-Stamm House
101 Hamilton Street
Architect: Cohen & Hacker
2011

Sited along the lakefront, this Contemporary residence combines natural and man-made materials in a fresh interpretation of the American Arts & Crafts idiom. Anchored at the corner by a three-story chimney of buff Wisconsin limestone, the house responds to the corner lot with carefully balanced expansive groupings of French doors and windows to provide sweeping panoramas of the park and lake. The harmony of the limestone base with the cedar-shingled sheathing on the other planes establishes the organic basis of the design. The angularity of the seamed metal roof is repeated in several gables and countered by the orthogonal vertical thrust of the second and third stories. The open floor plan, raised stone terrace and rooftop deck allow optimal interplay between interior and exterior spaces. Designed for clients active in the natural environment, Cohen and Hacker transformed fundamental architectural and organic allegories into modern prose. **KH**

Appendix A: Parks & Open Spaces

It might be said that Philo Judson, hired by Northwestern University to plat the village of Evanston, is the founder of Evanston's public park system. In 1853-54 he set aside areas for parks and the university campus, including the open space that we know today as Fountain Square. In 1882 Northwestern deeded lakefront land between Lake and Church Streets for the city's first public park.

In the 1880s Evanston resident Volney Foster, known as "The Father of Sheridan Road," promoted the building of a pleasure drive between Chicago and Milwaukee along the Lake Michigan shore. He formed the Sheridan Road Association and helped to reclaim land from the lakefront and establish parks along the drive.

In 1900, Frank Elliot donated over 7 acres of his property–from Lee to Hamilton streets along the lakefront–for a park, now named Elliot Park. In 1911 a number of prominent landowners donated the land at Greenwood Street for a park. As a result, the city passed an ordinance that set aside the land south of the university and north of Greenleaf Street for public parks.

Clark Street Beach, ca.1900
Photo: Northwestern University Archives

The Plan of Evanston was presented in 1917. Despite the land set aside for parks as noted above, the plan committee–composed of Dwight Perkins, Thomas Tallmadge, Daniel Burnham, Jr. and Hubert Burnham–intended to address the need for more park space along the lakefront.

In 1927 the Evanston Plan Commission parks committee, under the chairmanship of Thomas Tallmadge, began a comprehensive plan to develop and beautify the lakefront. Due to financial constraints at the time, only the seawall at Calvary Cemetery was built.

On July 4, 1929, an $8,000 flagstaff memorializing Evanston's war dead was dedicated at Patriots Park at Forest Place and Sheridan Road. The flagstaff base was designed by Thomas Tallmadge and executed by sculptor Stephen Beames.

The chain of Evanston lakefront parks is, by any standard, the jewel in the Evanston park system. For decades it has been the Lake Michigan lakefront that attracts residents and visitors alike to its magnetic charms.

The lakefront park system includes parks from north to south. Lawson Park at Sheridan Road and Clinton Place includes Noah's Playground for Everyone, an accessible playground giving opportunities to all children, no matter their physical circumstances. Moving south, lakefront parks include Centennial between Church and University Place, Dawes between Dempster and Church, Burnham Shores between Dempster and Hamilton, Elliott between Hamilton and Lee, Garden, north of Sheridan Square, and South Boulevard, Sheridan Square to the city limits.

At the lakefront, Evanston's five public swimming beaches are open seven days a week during the beach season. Three are accessible to people with disabilities: Lighthouse, Greenwood Street and Lee Street.

Dawes Park Lagoon, 2012
Photo: walkscore.com

Evanston has two boat launch facilities: the Church Street Powerboat Ramp and the Dempster Street Launch Facility for canoes, kayaks and sailboats. Windsurfers launch from Greenwood beach.

One of the newest parks in the Evanston park system is Lovelace Park, located at Gross Point Road just south of the Wilmette border. Previously a gravel pit and refuse dump site, the park was completed in 1980 and dedicated to Walter Lovelace, former managing editor of the *Evanston News-Index* and editor of the *Evanston Review*. Fishing programs for children are sponsored at the park's pond.

The nine-acre Twiggs Park near Simpson and the North Shore Channel was dedicated in 1986. At its eastern terminus at Green Bay Road the park features a bike path that connects to the North Shore Channel bike path and continues into Chicago along the North Branch of the Chicago River.

Dwight Perkins Woods is the only Cook County Forest Preserve parcel located in Evanston. Surrounded by a residential area on four sides, Perkins Woods is popular with joggers and walkers. The only man-made features of the preserve are paths that connect the four corners to a central meeting place.

Today the City of Evanston Parks Division provides the maintenance of all public grounds within the City. Over 300 acres of land, encompassing 97 sites, are managed by the City. These sites include 76 parks and 50 playgrounds. In addition to these, Lighthouse Park District in the northeast controls 3 parks and Ridgeville Park District on the south side controls 8 parks. JW

Appendix B: Cultural and Commercial Landmarks

When we think of landmarks we generally think of historically or architecturally significant buildings. Many of the 150 places in this book fall into these categories. A few do not. Institutions can be culturally important to a community without occupying a significant building or place. Longtime retail or service providers, too, can develop into a unifying element of a neighborhood or a shared memory of a city. Every resident of Evanston has a personal list of landmarks, of places that are significant in his or her life. We acknowledge here a very few of the many places that come to mind as part of our collective perception and the history of Evanston.

Photo: Unknown

Lemoi Ace Hardware
1008 Davis Street
Lemoi originated as a sheet metal repair shop (Peterson-Lemoi) in 1894 on the site that became the Chandler's Building. Peter Lemoi wanted a more mainstream retail operation and launched Lemoi Hardware, Evanston's oldest retail business still in operation, in 1895. Today, under the stewardship of fourth generation family member and president Ralph Lemoi Dupuis, Lemoi is thriving. Ralph's great grandfather, Peter, and grandfather, Ralph, are pictured in this photo.

Crystal Table Water
2318 Ridge Avenue
This bottled water company was started in 1896 when natural springs, still present, were discovered in the back yard of this house built in 1887. Crystal Table Water was bottled onsite and sold on the North Shore for over 70 years.

Photo: Flickr

The Toy Tinkers, Incorporated
805 Greenwood Street
In the early 1910s, Charles Pajeau designed the first Tinkertoy set in his garage after watching children play with pencils, sticks and empty spools of thread. Pajeau and his partner, Robert Pettit, introduced the new toy at the 1914 American Toy Fair and a year later over a million sets were sold; in 1947 they produced over 2.5 million. Gabriel Industries acquired the Tinkertoy line and moved operations to Maryland in 1978.

Evanston Sanitarium and Training School (LL)

1916–1918 Asbury Avenue

Dr. Isabella Garnett, a member of one of Evanston's first African-American families, started the Evanston Sanitarium and Training School in 1914 to care for the growing African-American community with her husband, Dr. Arthur Butler. Prior to this, since neither Evanston Hospital nor St. Francis Hospital would admit African-Americans, patients had to travel to the south or west side of Chicago for treatment. In 1930 the Community Hospital of Evanston replaced the Sanitarium in a brick house at 2026 Brown Avenue. Evanston's two exclusively white hospitals began to admit African-American patients in the 1950s. The Community Hospital, which had expanded to a larger location in 1952, closed in 1980.

Fanny's

1601 Simpson Street

Fanny's Restaurant, started in 1946, was a notable Evanston eatery cited by Chicago Magazine as one of the top 40 Chicago-area restaurants ever. Patrons included the Marshall Field family. The salad dressing and meat sauce won international acclaim and are still available today. The restaurant closed in 1987 due to the health of its founder, Fanny Bianucci. The building was converted to lofts in 2005.

Photo: Charles Seton

Amazingrace

Chicago Avenue & Main Street

Amazingrace started as a coffeehouse in Northwestern University's Scott Hall in 1971 and immediately became a focus for music. The collective hosted such greats as the Grateful Dead, John Prine, Keith Jarrett, Sonny Rollins, McCoy Tyner and nearby Evanston resident Steve Goodman (in photo). In 1974 a loyal group of "Gracers" created a new Amazingrace at The Main in south Evanston. Amazingrace became an icon of the youth culture of the times and closed after its short but vibrant life in 1978.

Bookman's Alley

1721 (Rear) Sherman Avenue

Bookman's Alley boasted 40,000 volumes and occupied an expansive one-story shed located off the alley connecting Sherman and Benson. The shop's unique ambiance came not just from its enormous selection of used books, but from its comfortable groupings of rugs, antique furniture and lamps, and the maps, paintings and posters hung on the few walls not covered with books. Roger Carlson opened the store in 1980. It closed in 2013. JW

Appendix C: Shopping and Cultural Districts

Served by rapid transit for over a century, Evanston's shopping and cultural districts were shaped by transit-oriented development of the 19th and 20th century and continue into the 21st. With easy access to Chicago via CTA and Metra, mixed use buildings, corporate headquarters, hospitals, specialty restaurants and eclectic shops developed along transit corridors to create the vibrant neighborhood shopping and cultural districts that we know today.

Photo: Laura Saviano

Centered at the **Main Street** stations of CTA and Metra, a rich mix of beloved retailers and cultural activities such as a not-for-profit arts center and an annual art and craft fair make the Main Street Shopping District a city destination. A professional "co-working" facility privides entrepreneurs with work and conference space. **Dempster Street** is home to over 60 eclectic shops, restaurants and cafes. Gift shops, art galleries and a venue offering live music and a recording studio lend a hip feel to the neighborhood. Several grocery stores located nearby create a "food corridor" for Evanston.

Photo: Wikipedia

Church Street is a vibrant area of retailers, residential buildings, corporate headquarters, churches, hotels, a 21-screen movie theater, restaurants and public buildings including the Evanston Public Library. This regional destination brings visitors from all over to Evanston. At **Noyes Street**, Evanston's Cultural Arts Center houses theater companies and offers art and acting classes to the community. Restaurants, cafes and grocery stores line both sides of this charming street; Evanston's City Hall and Northwestern University are close by.

Photo: GoogleMaps

Along the northern edge of the city, **Central Street** is served by both Metra and CTA. The busy street connects art galleries, antique stores, specialty shops, restaurants, bakeries and a Native American museum, and ends at the Evanston Art Center on Lake Michigan.

Evanston's larger shopping centers are located at **Howard, Main and Oakton Streets** near McCormick Boulevard. Evanston Center, on our southern border at Howard and Kedzie, generates the city's greatest sales tax revenue with its large-scale retailers. An award-winning national branch bank is located here. Further east, near the Howard CTA station, a developing commercial district has restaurants, specialty stores and entertainment venues. Main Street Commons at Main and McCormick is home to large national retailers and smaller specialty shops. Oakton Street offers a large do-it-yourself home goods store, grocery stores, a restaurant and a national pet store.

The west side's **Dempster/Dodge** shopping district is the historic industrial corridor that was home to a steel mill, brickyards and railroad infrastructure including the Mayfair line. **"WestEnd"** is evolving with entrepreneurial spirit: small commercial, light manufacturing, artists and artisans–many in live/work lofts–have moved in. A few blocks east of Dodge, **Florence Avenue** now offers a café, studios and a letterpress print shop, and was once home to butchers, bakers and other shops that served Eastern European immigrants working in Evanston's west side factories.

At **Church and Dodge**, near Evanston Township High School, a mix of retail and cultural establishments have served the west side for many decades. A new "cultural café" offers dance and fitness classes, a computer lab, recording studio and performance space. A beloved barber shop is an unofficial community and social center.

The Dr. Hill neighborhood at **Simpson and Green Bay** is named for Dr. Elizabeth Webb Hill, an Evanstonian dedicated to providing medical care to the African-American community. This is another area that has reclaimed former industrial spaces; the neighborhood features offices, live/work studios and a culinary incubator.

The walkable atmosphere and quality of life that these diverse and vibrant shopping and cultural districts offer make Evanston both a suburb and a city unto itself. LS

Appendix D: New Deal Art in Evanston

It is commonly assumed that all public art commissioned by the federal government during the Depression was sponsored by the Works Progress Administration, or WPA. In fact, four New Deal art programs operated during this time. It all began when artist George Biddle wrote to President Franklin Roosevelt to say that artists were in need of economic relief as much as anyone else; this led to the first program, the Public Works of Art Project (1933–34). As that ended the U.S. Treasury Section of Painting and Sculpture filled the void from 1934–1939, when it became the Section of Fine Art. Both are simply referred to as "the Section." The Section awarded commissions on a project basis–funded by 1% of the building cost–and was regional in nature, stressing local color and ideals of community, democracy and hard work. Conventional art was favored to appeal to the broadest audience.

The Federal Arts Project, under the WPA, began in 1935. It employed artists on a salary, primarily to create art for schools, hospitals and libraries, and did not limit work to representational art. Abstract artist Jackson Pollock was one well-known artist who benefited from the FAP. The Section and the FAP were reorganized in 1939 under the Federal Works Agency; all art programs ended in 1942–1943. Artists in these programs spoke of an uplift to morale and of the sense of being at last acknowledged as an important member of the social family, with a place in the economic system.

In Evanston, numerous examples of New Deal art were installed, and many still exist.

All photos: wpamurals.com

The Section emphasized art in post offices since these buildings were a key link to the federal government and used by all citizens in a community. In 1938 our Main Post Office was awarded two pairs of sculptures: Robert I. Russin's "Throwing the Mail" and "Mail Handler," 7-foot tall cast aluminum figures covered with 23-carat gold foil, and Armin A. Scheler's carved limestone reliefs over the entry doors entitled "The Message" and "The Answer." These sculptures embody the heroic ideal typical of much Section art.

Evanston's public schools became home to many pieces of New Deal art due to the ardent sponsorship of Frederick Nichols, Evanston's Superintendent of Schools and Secretary of the Board of Education during the New Deal and a member of the FAP's citizen's advisory board. Unfortunately, many the works have disappeared during renovations or repairs. A selection of the remaining works follow.

"The Organ Grinder," by George Orloff, is a watercolor painting at Washington School said to depict a real organ grinder who performed in downtown Evanston.

"Negro Children," "Band Playing" and "Dance Scene" are oil paintings at Nichols School by Harlem Renaissance painter Archibald Motley, Jr., one of the very few African-American artists sponsored by the New Deal. It was thought that the racial diversity of the school and neighborhood were the reason for Motley's inclusion and subject matter.

At Oakton School, pinewood bas reliefs by Alfred Lenzi remain, entitled "Animals," "Farm Animals" and "Wild Animals of America." Carl Scheffler and Ethel Spears painted "Charlemagne," a series of recently restored murals.

Anyone entering Haven School has passed four 6-ft Bedford limestone sculptures of children by Mary Anderson Mott. Each child is in a contemplative mood and accompanied by a companion animal. In the entry hall are "9 Portrait Circles," oak bas reliefs by Louise Pain.

Haven's riches continue with Carl Scheffler's "Old Lady in the Shoe" and "Cinderella" murals in the main floor hallway.

Although not specific to Evanston, further examples of New Deal art are preserved in the collection of Northwestern University's Mary and Leigh Block Museum. HH

Appendix E: Mail-order Homes

The Evanston houses listed here have been identified by historical architectural researcher Rebecca Hunter as very likely to be mail-order homes. Confirmed mail-order houses are noted with an asterisk.

Model	Address	Company
Westly	1733 Brown	Sears
Clyde	1801 Brown	Sears
Lynhaven	912 Brown	Sears
Lynhaven	2021 Brown	Sears
Unknown *	1405 Brummel	Sears
Verona *	2815 Colfax	Sears
Berwyn	2336 Cowper	Sears
Unknown	1611 Dodge	?
Rodessa	2046 Dodge	Sears
1510	1815 Emerson	Harris Bros
Westly	2315 Emerson	Sears
Alden *	2108 Harrison	Sears
Berwyn	3242 Harrison	Sears
Mitchell	3304 Harrison	Sears
Collingwood	2103 Maple	?
Colchester *	2000 Noyes	Sears
Barrington	3012 Park Pl	Sears
Ardara *	2405 Payne	Sears
Argyle	2407 Payne	Sears
Argyle *	2105 Pioneer	Sears
Lustron 02	2320 Prospect	Lustron
1502	2411 Prospect	Harris Bros
Normandy	2412 Prospect	Sears
Van Dorn	2437 Prospect	Sears
Van Dorn	2441 Prospect	Sears
Vallonia	2507 Prospect	Sears
522	2321 Ridgeway	Gordon-Van Tine
Osborn	2430 Ridgeway	Sears
Osborn	2121 Simpson	Sears
Osborn	2421 Simpson	Sears
Kilbourne	2436 Simpson	Sears
Martha Washington	3340 Thayer	Sears
Belmont	1008 Wesley	Sears

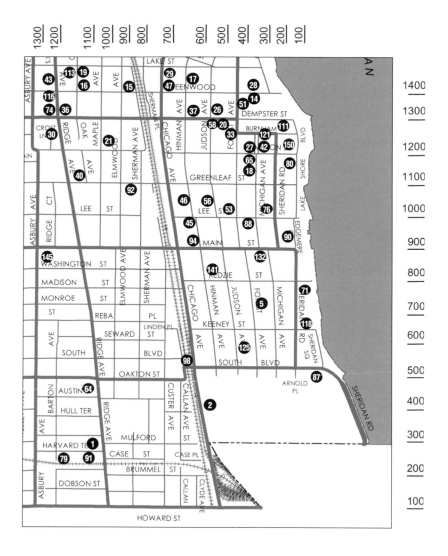

● Refers to page number in book

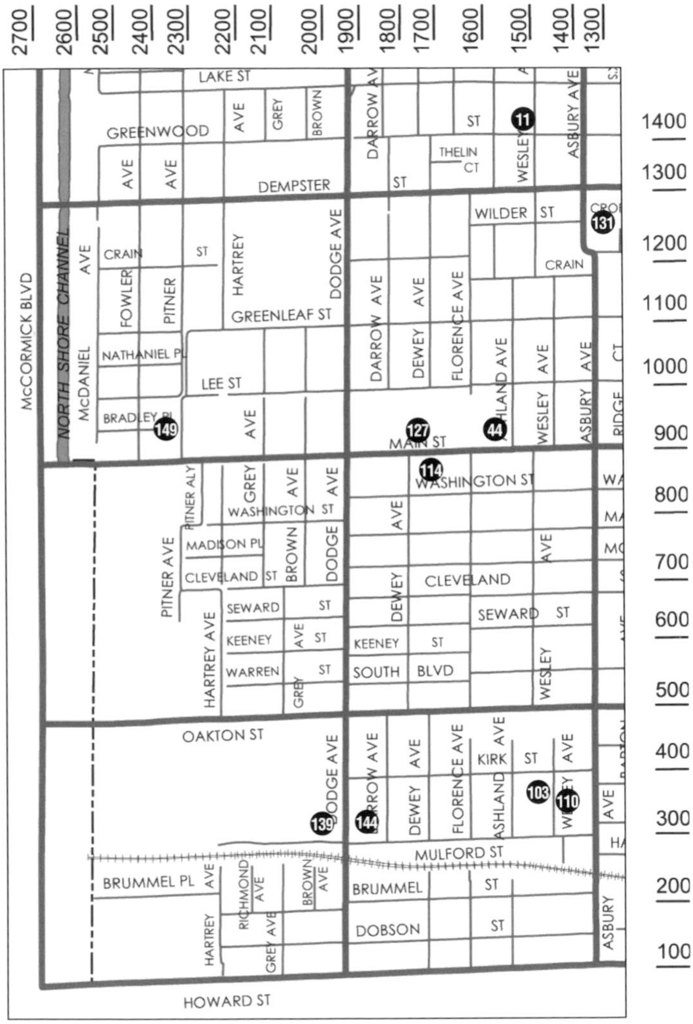

❶ Refers to page number in book

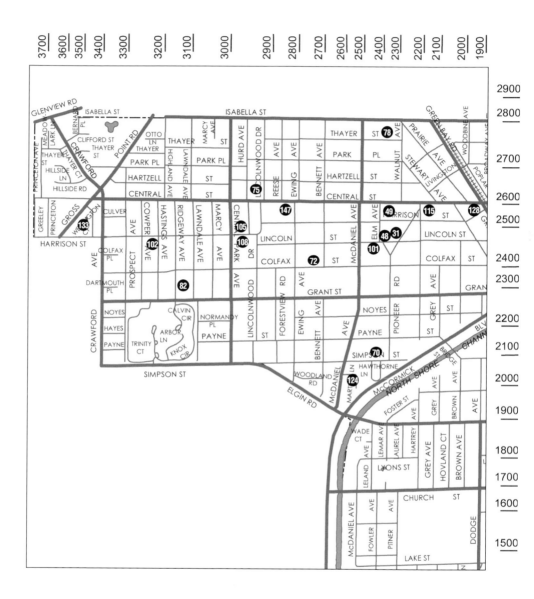

❶ Refers to page number in book

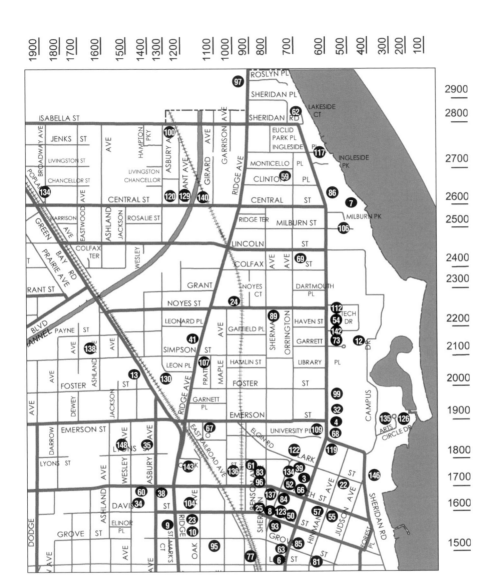

● Refers to page number in book

Selected Bibliography

Anderson, Jon. "David Haid, Award-winning Architect," Chicago Tribune, March 3, 1993.

Andreotti, Margherita, Ph.D. with Christine Bell, Ph.D. and Nancy Flannery. *Preliminary Survey of Historic Art in Evanston*, City of Evanston, Evanston IL, 2007.

Bach, Ira J. *Guide to Chicago's Historic Suburbs*. Swallow Press/Ohio UniversityPress. Chicago IL, 1981.

Benjamin, Susan and Evanston Preservaton Commission. *Suburban Apartment Buildings in Evanston, Illinois*. National Register of Historic Places Nomination. Evanston IL, 1983.

Benjamin, Susan, Editor. *An Architectural Album: Chicago's North Shore*. The Junior League of Evanston. Evanston IL, 1988.

Blum, Betty J., Interviewer. *Interview with Bertram A. Weber; Interview with William Keck*. Chicago Architects Oral History Project, The Art Institute of Chicago. Chicago IL, 1983; 1990.

Buchbinder-Green, Barbara J. *Evanston: A Pictorial History*. G. Bradley Publishing, Inc. St. Louis MO, 1989.

Buchbinder-Green, Barbara J. and Anne O. Earle. *Evanston Ridge Historic District*. Natioonal Register of Historic Places Nomination. Evanston IL, 1982.

Burnette, Mark, Judy Fiske, Jeanne Lindwall, Jim McGuire, and Mary McWilliams. *Northeast Evanston Historic District*. National Register of Historic Places Nomination. Northeast Evanston Historic District Association. Evanston IL, 1999.

Clement, Russell with Jeffrey Garrett and Janet Olson. *Deering Library, An Illustrated History*. Northwestern University Library. Evanston IL, 2008.

Cohen, Stuart and Susan Benjamin. *North Shore Chicago: Houses of the Lakefront Suburbs 1890-1940*. Acanthus Press, New York NY, 2004.

Core, Dublin. *The Work of Bertram A. Weber, A.I.A., Architect, Chicago, Illinois*. Architecture and Design Vol. IV, No. 9, April 1940.

"The Cranford Doll Houses" House Beautiful, Volume 7, No. 6, November 1900.

Dell'Angela, Tracy. "Laverne Strickland: Black Hospitals Held Out Hope At A Time When White Hospitals Shut The Doors," Chicago Tribune, November 17, 1996.

"The Depression Era Art Projects in Illinois," lib.niu.edu/2000.

"Dismantling a Legacy: New Deal Post Offices for Sale," savethepostoffices.com/new-deal-post-offices, 2013.

Earle, Anne O. and Mary B. McWilliams. *Historic Evanston Architecture: Four Walking Tours of the Ridge and Lakeshore Historic Districts*. Evanston Planning & Zoning Department and Evanston Preservation Commission. Evanston IL, 1993.

Ebner, Michael H. *Creating Chicago's North Shore*. The University of Chicago Press. Chicago IL, 1988.

"Evanston Women's History Project Biographies," evanstonforever.org/community/womenshistoryproject.html

Evrailfan with Bob Guhr and Hank Morris. 150 Years on the Rail, "The Junction Railroad Company." trainweb.org, 2013.

"Federal Art Programs," gsa.gov, 2013.

"Federal Art Project," wikipedia.com, 2013.

Gardner, Barbara. *The Proposed Oakton Historic District*. Evanston IL, October 2003.

Gardner, Barbara and Jack Weiss. *Oakton Historic District*. National Register of Historic Places Nomination. Oakton Historic District Committee. Evanston IL, 2004.

Gordon, Eleanor. "Art Deco," North Shore Magazine, May/June 1977.

Gottschalk, Paul and Eden Juron Pearlman, exhibition curators. *Evanston Through the Eyes of an Artist: Forty Years of Evanston Paintings by Walter Burt Adams*. Evanston Historical Society and Evanston Public Library. Evanston IL, 2000.

Granacki Historic Consultants. *Architectural Resources in the Lakeshore Historic District. Evanston, Illinois*. Chicago IL, 2012.

Grese, Robert E. *Jens Jensen, Maker of Natural Parks and Gardens*. The Johns Hopkins University Press, Baltimore MD, 1998.

Heise, Kenan. "Bertram Weber, Architect for 64 Years," Chicago Tribune, December 19, 1989.

Hillier, Bevis. *Art Deco of the 20s and 30s*. Studio Vista. London, 1968.

Hurd, Harvey B. and Robert D. Sheppard, editors. *History of Northwestern University and Evanston*. Library of Congress, Washington D.C., December 31, 1906.

Kellogg, Florence Loeb. "Art Becomes Public Works," Survey Graphic, Vol.23, No.6., Survey Associates, June 1934.

Loftis, Dean. "Planting Some Drama," Chicago Tribune, April 3, 2010.

Lowe, David. *Lost Chicago*. Houghton Mifflin Company, Boston MA, 1978.

Mahoney, Elenor. "The Great Depression in Washington State," depts.washington.edu, 2012.

McAlester, Virginia and Lee McAlester. *Field Guide to American Houses*. Knopf Doubleday Publishing Group, New York NY, 1984.

Moss, Roger, Executive Editor. *Small Houses of the Twenties: The Sears, Roebuck 1926 House Catalog*. Dover Publications, Inc., Mineola NY, 1991.

Obermaier, Dan. "Keck Brothers Bring Mid-Century Modern Home." jetsetmodern.com, 2000.

Perkins, Margery Blair. *Evanstonia: An Informal History of Evanston and Its Architecture*. Compiled and edited by Barbara J. Buchbinder-Green. Evanston Historical Society, Evanston IL. Chicago Review Press, Chicago IL, 1984.

Peterson, Mimi. *Postcard History Series: Evanston.* Arcadia Publishing, Charleston SC, 2008.

Pridmore, Jay. *Northwestern University: The Campus Guide.* Princeton Architectural Press, New York NY, 2009.

Rodkin, Dennis. "Modernist Home of Architect Who Designed Ferris Bueller's 'Garage'," chicagomag.com, March 5, 2012.

Schulze, Franz. *Illinois Institute of Technology: Campus Guide.* Princeton Architectural Press. New York NY, 2005.

Small Houses of the Twenties, The Sears, Roebuck 1926 House Catalog. Dover Publications, Inc. Mineola, NY, 1991.

Spencer, Robert. "'The Doll's House' and Two Others," The House Beautiful, Volume.10, November 1901.

Storrer, William Allin. *The Architecture of Frank Lloyd Wright: A Complete Catalog. Updated 3rd Edition.* The University of Chicago Press. London, 2007.

Terras, Donald J. *The Grosse Point Lighthouse.* Windy City Press, Evanston IL, 1995.

"T.E. Tallmadge Funeral Today: Killed in Wreck," Chicago Daily Tribune, January 3, 1940

Wilson, Anne. *Beyond Architecture: Marion Mahony and Walter Burley Griffin: America, Australia and India.* Powerhouse Publishing. Sydney, Australia. 1998.

Wolfe, Peg. "Evanston Garden 'Staycation," examiner.com, July 18, 2010.

Selected Websites

artic.edu
artic.edu/research/bertrand-goldberg-archive
bahai.us
bertrandgoldberg.org
blockmuseum.northwestern.edu/view/collections/prints-drawings.html
christianscience.org
cinematreasures.org/theaters/418
cityofchicago.org/landmarksweb/web/home.htm
cityofevanston.org/assets/ReportEvschoolartillustration.pdf
cityofevanston.org/assets/reportEvschoolartTEXT.pdf
cityofevanston.org/evanston-life/history-demographics/
cityofevanston.org/parks-recreation/
cornellcollege.edu/cornell-report/issues/2011-spring/article2/page-2.shtml
designevanston.org/documents/downtownevanstonrevitalized07.pdf
digital.library.northwestern.edu/architecture/building.php?bid=26
digital.library.northwestern.edu/architecture/campus.php?campus=2
en.wikipedia.org/wiki/List_of_Northwestern_University_buildings
epl.org/adams/top.html
evanston150.org/home

evanstonedge.com

faithatfirst.com/?page_id=3053

firstpresevanston.org/about-us/history-0

georgemaher.com

graveyards.com/IL/cook/calvary/

illinoishsglorydays.com/id802.html

jetsetmodern.com

kithouse.org/

landmarkhunter.com/scripts/search.cgi?query=Evanston+IL

library.northwestern.edu/libraries-collections/evanston-campus/university-archives/
    evanston-property-history

lifeofanarchitect.com/women-in-architecture/

livingplaces.com/IL/Cook_County/Evanston_City.html

lynnbecker.com/repeat/Mahony/mahony.htm

maps.northwestern.edu

midcenturia.com/2011/01/ben-rose-house

nl.edu

peterbeers.net/interests/flw_rt/Illinois/Illinois.htm

pickstaiger.org

prairieschooltraveler.com/html/il/evanston/evanston.html

prairiestyles.com/

robertseyfartharchitect.com

savethepostoffices.com/new-deal-post-offices

secondbaptistevanston.org/content.cfm?id=296

shorefrontlegacy.org

southeastevanstonassociation.org

stmaryevanston.org/Parish/History.html

tclf.org

thefranklloydwrighttour.com/

thelowreygroup.com/single-family-residential/italian-villa-style-architecture/

undereverystone.blogspot.com/

voices.yahoo.com/tinker-toys-where-all-began-6891.html?cat=46

wikipedia.org

wikipedia.org/wiki/Art_Deco

wikipedia.org/wiki/Post_Office_Murals

wpamurals.com

wpamurals.com/evanston.html

youtube.com/watch?v=JOdH_SZTfkI

Index by Place Name

Warren House, 62

Washington School, 44

White House, 36

Willard House, 3

Will House, 105

Wilson House, 125

The Woman's Club of Evanston, 66

Zecher House, 91

Index by Street Name

1014 Hinman Avenue, 46
1433 Hinman Avenue, 17
1445 Hinman Avenue, 81
1635-41 Hinman/418-20 Church, 55
1745 Hinman Avenue, 22

580 Ingleside Park, 117

529 Judson Avenue, 125
1024 Judson Avenue, 56
1243–49 Judson/326–28 Dempster, 58
1301–03/1305–07 Judson Avenue, 26

607 Lake Street, 6
1012 Lake Street, 19
Lake Street and Oak Avenue, 113
1140 Lake Shore Boulevard, 80
502–12 Lee/936–40 Hinman, 45
640 Lincoln Street, 69
2319 Lincoln Street, 48
2418 Lincoln Street, 101
2614 Lincolnwood Drive, 75

501–07 Main/904–08 Hinman, 94
1216 Main Street, 145
1616-1708 Main/847 Dewey, 114
1701 Main Street, 127
1209-1217 Maple Avenue, 21
17 Martha Lane, 124
840 Michigan Avenue, 132
940-950 Michigan Avenue, 88
1144 Michigan Avenue, 18
1201–13 Michigan/205–07 Hamilton, 42
1221 Michigan Avenue, 121
2–12 Milburn Park, 106

718–734 Noyes Street, 89
927 Noyes Street, 24

1100 and 1106 Oak Avenue, 40
1401 Oak Avenue, 16

1500 Oak Avenue, 10
1560 Oak Avenue, 23
1740 Oak Avenue, 143
1601 Orrington Avenue, 123
1703 Orrington Avenue, 52, 134
2636 Orrington Avenue, 59

2444-2450 Pioneer Road, 31
940 Pitner Street, 149

250 Ridge Avenue, 1
436 Ridge Avenue, 64
1232 Ridge Avenue, 30
1307–13 Ridge Avenue, 36
1314 Ridge Avenue, 74
1330 Ridge Avenue, 116
1426 Ridge Avenue, 43
1514 Ridge Avenue, 9
2049 Ridge Avenue, 107
2100 Ridge Avenue, 41
2301–2319 Ridgeway Avenue, 82

470–498 Sheridan Road, 87
747 Sheridan Road, 71
1000 Sheridan Road, 76
1801 Sheridan Road, 146
1870 Sheridan Road, 119
1881 Sheridan Road, 68
1897 Sheridan Road, 4
1935 Sheridan Road, 99
2121 Sheridan Road, 73
2133 Sheridan Road, 142
2145 Sheridan Road, 54, 112
2535 Sheridan Road, 7
2603 Sheridan Road, 86
2840 Sheridan Road, 97
2829 Sheridan Place, 62
647 Sheridan Square, 118
1580 Sherman Avenue, 137
1700 Sherman Avenue, 96
1710 Sherman Avenue, 83

Index by Architect Name

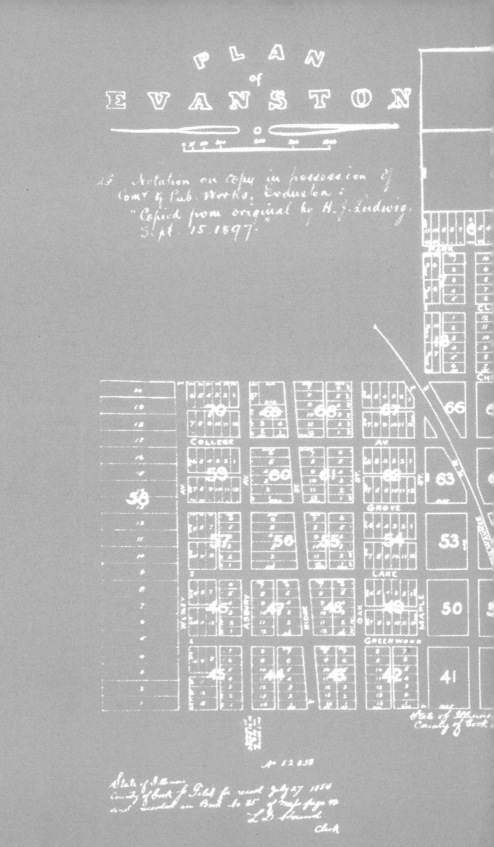